THE LIVING HAND

A highly original guide to hand reading offering much that is new and revolutionary.

By the same author:
FORTUNE TELLING BY TAROT CARDS (Sasha Fenton)

THE Living Hand

A unique guide to modern hand analysis

SASHA FENTON and MALCOLM WRIGHT

THE AQUARIAN PRESS
Wellingborough, Northamptonshire

First published 1986

British Library Cataloguing in Publication Data

Fenton, Sasha
   The living hand: a unique guide to modern
hand analysis.
   1. Palmistry
   I. Title   II. Wright, Malcolm
   133.6   BF921

ISBN 0-85030-514-4

The Aquarian Press is part of the Thorsons Publishing Group

Printed and bound in Great Britain

Contents

Dedicated to Elizabeth and Rebecca Wright, also Helen and Stuart Fenton.

Acknowledgements

Grateful thanks to Tony Fenton for all his liaison work and Kay Bielecki for checking the typescript. Thanks also to hand readers Sheila McGuirk, John Lindsay and Ashwin Pandya who contributed information and experimented with some of our ideas.

Introduction

We have written this book for those who are interested in hand reading and want a more up to date approach to the subject. The ideas presented here have come directly from our own experience of working with hands. We have attempted to explain how character and personality can be read and how this information can be constructively used by the reader to understand his own nature and to help others to get to grips with theirs in order to get more out of life. Incidentally, we have decided for the sake of convenience to use the masculine terms of 'he' and 'him' throughout this book. We have no preference for either sex, we believe in 'people's lib'.

History of Hand Analysis

Hand analysis, more commonly known as palmistry, goes back to the dawn of time, and the truly amazing thing is that so many hand readers from different cultures and different centuries actually agree on so many aspects of hand analysis. One of those who gave birth to modern methods was Casimir Stanislas d'Arpentigny who classified hand shapes into the now famous types of spatulate, square, elementary, conic, psychic, philosophic and mixed. The French nobleman Adrien Adolphe Desbarrolles had a mystical view of hand reading which he wrapped up with other occult ideas. He gave daily consultations in his apartment in the strangely named Rue d'Enfer (Road of Hell!). He also studied graphology and phrenology and was deeply convinced that the Kabbala was the centre of all wisdom and guidance for the soul, mind and body.

Another famous name in palmistry was Count Louis Hamon (1866–1936), better known as Cheiro, who studied hand analysis for over forty years, along with other occult research work, such as numerology and astrology. He taught, lectured, travelled widely in Europe and America, amazing the VIPs of his day with the accuracy of his readings.

Clairvoyance

Hand analysis is a science and does not need to rely on intuition. People who want to read the hands of others, as opposed to just learning about themselves, will find themselves developing intuitively as well as developing a knowledge of psychology and human behaviour. The actual act of hand reading requires that one sits with the client in a quiet room building up a relaxed and trusting atmosphere. This is as conducive to building up clairvoyant faculties as meditation and yoga. It is not possible to work as a professional hand reader without learning to understand people; and in time, even the most 'scientific' hand reader learns to use that inexplicable intuitive 'nudge' which comes while working on a hand.

Interpretation

Hands vary much more than one imagines and there must be some leeway for interpretation. Skilled hand analysts *do* have varying interpretations, in the same way that astrologers vary in their opinions. In some cases we ourselves have different ways of interpreting the same lines or different ways of coming to the same conclusion and, where that occurs, we give both our opinions.

Some lines give information on more than one aspect of one's life, in the same way that a sign of the Zodiac can encompass a wide variety of ideas within itself. These lines will have to be read carefully with due attention being paid to other parts of the hand. Wherever we have to deal with this kind of problem we will give a detailed cross reference — we will not just say vaguely 'other areas of the hand will have to be looked at'.

Beginners and advanced hand readers alike will find something to interest them in our book because the information within it ranges from the basics to the most advanced techniques. We have not tried to turn traditional palmistry on its head, indeed we have followed the traditional ideas where we have found them to work well. Any of our methods which differ from the usual ones have been meticulously researched over a period of time. In the case of methods which are so new that they have not had time to be conclusively researched, we are throwing these over to you, the reader, to test against your own clients. We make a point of explaining our reasoning so that the reader can see the logic behind the new theories. We hope that our departures from the traditional and 'official' line will bring many hours of happy argument and research to the world of hand analysis.

Illustrations

Up to now many hand-reading books have been spoiled by the fact that they have either been illustrated by artists who are not hand readers or hand readers who cannot draw, but in this book we are lucky to be able to draw upon Malcolm's background and knowledge. Thankfully, he not only has many years of hand-reading experience behind him but also a long career as a technical illustrator. In addition to being an illustrator, he is also a creative artist who has successfully sold his own paintings.

Each illustration has been carefully prepared to give a clear and accurate picture, often backed up by hand prints, in order to show precisely what we have described in the text. All the diagrams are drawn as if looking at the right hand print of a right handed person. The inked prints are all right hand unless otherwise stated.

We hope that you will now take up our book, give yourself time to absorb the ideas and gradually work your way through the case histories. This book should give you a thorough grounding in the art (or is it science?) of hand analysis.

How to Take Prints

Equipment required

Water based printing ink, available from art shops.

Rubber roller, also from an art shop.

Ceramic tile.

Paper kitchen towel.

Plain white paper — a cheap unlined A4 note pad is ideal.

An old rolling pin.

Method

Squeeze a little of the ink onto the tile and then roll it onto the roller. Lightly roll off any excess onto the kitchen towel. Gently roll the ink onto the hand being careful not to press it deeply into the lines on the hand. Place the hand on the paper and press gently so that all of the hand is in contact with the paper. If the hand is very hollow in the middle, then place the paper on the rolling pin and roll the hand over it. This will distort the appearance of the fingers, therefore it would be a good idea to do one set of prints with the roller and one without, thereby getting the whole of the palm on paper and also having a separate set of prints with the fingers correctly shown. Alternatively, experiment with hard and soft surfaces placed under the paper.

CHAPTER ONE

The Hand at a Glance:

Basic Information

When a palmist looks at a pair of hands he can see a picture of a person's whole life at a glance. He can tell about character, aptitudes and potential for success or failure in every sphere of life. He can spot a potential hazard and warn the subject accordingly.

Our hands are constantly changing, reflecting at any one time our state of health, state of mind, past events and the likely course of future ones. **Lines can and do change from time to time**; the hand is part of the living body which is why we have decided to think of it as a 'living hand'.

Size of Hands

The hands should be in proportion to the size of the body. If they are exceptionally large, the subject may be very slow and cautious; if very small either very fast moving and excitable or totally idle. Either way there will be an imbalance in the personality and probably an unhappy nature.

Hand Shapes

These give an 'at a glance' clue to character. One should let common sense be one's guide — a large square, heavily calloused hand is hardly likely to belong to a budding Nureyev! More about this in Chapter 2.

The Mounts (Fig. 1.1)

This is the basic 'map' of the palm. The areas, known as mounts, each have their own characteristic. This a brief introduction to the mounts.

Jupiter	Ambition, application of will power, dignity, financial drive, religious and philosophic outlook.
Saturn	Practicalities, work, materialism, responsibility, search for truth, science.
Apollo	Home, relationships, hobbies, arts and crafts, self-expression.
Mercury	Communications, business, health, relationships, family, interests, diplomacy, honesty.
Lower Mars	Military matters, courage, resistance.
Upper Mars	Courage, temper, resilience, persistence; restlessness, drive.
Venus	Home, family, love, music, art, possessions, values, sensuality, stamina.
Neptune	Link between conscious and unconscious, health, intuition.

Luna   Travel, imagination, intuition, outdoor hobbies, freedom.

Each finger draws energy from its adjacent mount.

Life   The way one lives, health, drive, location of home, travel, efforts and failures.

Head   The mind, mental and physical health, career, education.

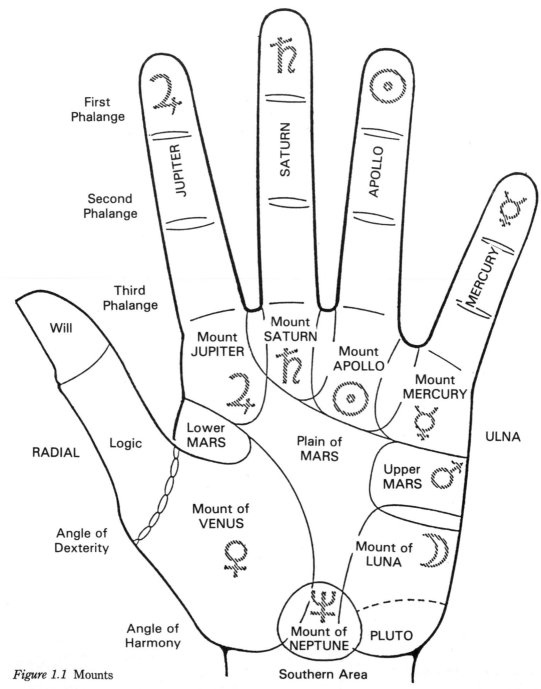

Figure 1.1 Mounts

Major Lines (Fig. 1.2)

Heart Health, feelings, sexuality, outlook on relationships.

Fate Work, earned money, partner- ships, successes and failures.

Apollo Home, family, hobbies, interests, arts, relationships.

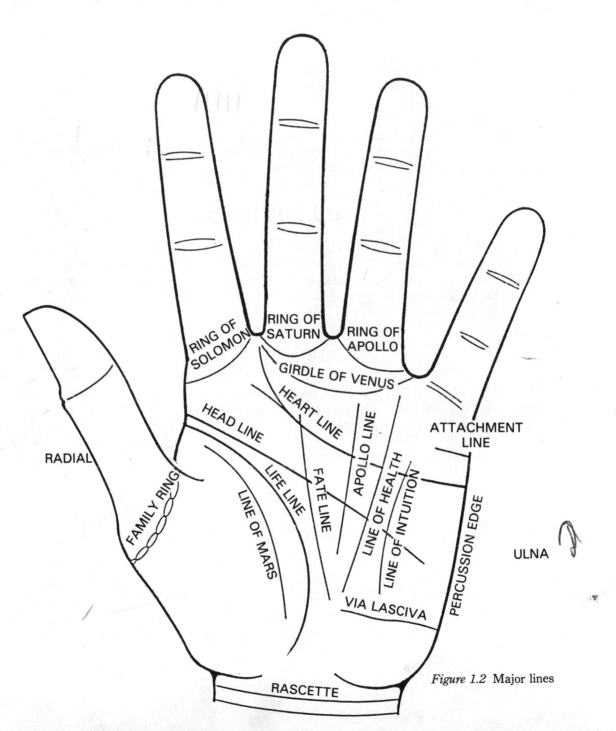

Figure 1.2 Major lines

Minor Lines

There are too many to go into detail in this section. Most people will have a few of these lines; it is not usual to have all of them. One or two common lines are the attachment/relationship lines, child lines and travel lines.

Marks

Crosses, grilles etc. The old-time palmists seem to have put a great deal of stock by these marks — we do not think that most of them are terribly important; however they do appear when something is on the subject's mind and some can be a valuable guide. Especially interesting ones are squares of restriction/protection and crosses of irritation. Other marks are actual patterns which lie under the skin, such as finger prints. These do not change much after adulthood and they give information on personality and particular talents.

Hard/Soft Hands

Firmness in hands indicates good health and a resourceful, self-reliant, tough personality, someone who is hard on himself and on others. Soft hands belong to gentler people who need to lean on others. Illness will make the hands soft, as will old age, pregnancy and vegetarianism. Hands that feel like a wet sponge trapped in a polythene bag show that something is very wrong.

Colour

Pale hands would indicate a limp and unenthusiastic personality whereas very red hands are traditionally supposed to mean bad temper. However, colour is mainly to do with health. Pale hands could indicate anaemia, yellow ones — jaundice, grey/blue ones — heart trouble, red patches on Luna — overactive thryoid or high blood-pressure, blue/white — poor circulation.

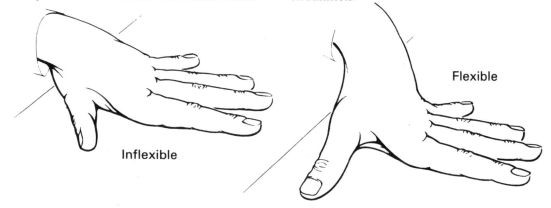

Inflexible

Flexible

Figure 1.3 Flexibility

Flexible hands are found on people who become bored easily; they need to have a stimulating job where they are offered a variety of problems and challenges plus plenty of sporting or social life. These people need to feel fairly free but are *not* necessarily particularly adaptable. The person whose fingers offer absolutely no resistance may be too dependent on the goodwill of others.

Inflexible hands show people who want a steady job and a quiet routine at home. They do not seek popularity and may be too unbending toward others. They cannot cope too well with unexpected events; they prefer to know where they are from one day to the next.

The Dominant Hand

'Length of days is in her right hand; and in her left hand riches and honour' *Proverbs* 3.16.

The gypsies in Spain charge one price to read one hand and double the amount to read both — but a reading with only one hand is a complete waste of time. The above quotation from *Proverbs* would be correct for a *right-handed person* because the length of days, plus the events which take place during those days, are marked on the right hand. The *inner* desires plus the *potential* for gaining riches and honour are marked on the left. One must establish which is the dominant, or major, hand; normally it is the one used to write with. In the case of a left-handed person both hands must be studied. Take note of any differences in the hands concerning events in the past, then give the interpretation of these events to the subject. The feedback from this gives a clue to the dominant hand. Sometimes more fine 'worry' lines can be seen on the minor hand than on the dominant one. Even armed with this information, it would be best to proceed with caution.

The dominant hand is reality. It is what we make of our lives plus our conscious self, the side we show to the outside world. It is also our achievements, the way we plan our lives, our changing views of relationships, work and money. It is the down-to-earth side of life. The major lines of Life, Head and Heart on the dominant hand also represent the physical organs of the body.

The Minor Hand

This hand represents our inner, unconscious self. This is the side which we hide from others. It could be called the 'I wish' hand because it represents our inner aspirations — the way we would like life to be rather than the reality we have to live with.

The lines of Life, Head and Heart on the minor hand represent the nervous, emotional and sexual energies of the body. This is where the build-up of nervous energies will appear before they arrive in the form of an impending physical illness on the dominant hand (see Chapter 12).

Marked Differences between Left and Right Hands

Marked differences between the hands can lead to mental, physical or sexual difficulties in life. For instance, if the heart line starts on the lower mount of Jupiter on one hand and between Saturn and Jupiter on the other, this person will always question love. He or she will have difficulties in understanding him or herself physically and psychologically. A rigid Saturn finger on the dominant hand and a flexible Saturn finger on the minor hand would imply a wish to be seen doing the right thing, and an inner desire to throw caution to the winds.

Differences in the formation of the head line between the two hands lead to a peculiar form of psychosis or split personality. In some cases the subject has trained himself to behave in a manner which is acceptable to his family or workmates while he is inwardly longing to act differently.

Size Differences

In many cases one hand, usually the dominant one, is larger than the other. This shows growth of confidence and capability due to coping with life. If the dominant hand is obviously squarer, it shows an increase in practicality during the subject's life.

There are cases where the lines on the minor hand show past experiences which appear to have been traumatic; despite the apparent scale of these events, the lines do not seem to appear on the dominant hand.

When these lines are pointed out to the subject and the possible course of past events is discussed, he usually confirms that there was an awfully bad patch in the past but he has put it behind him now and cannot really recall the pain of it any more. This is quite normal as the memory *must* become insensitive to painful past events for the sake of mental health. We may learn from the past, but cannot go through life with the pain undiminished — the hands show this.

Full Hands (Fig. 1.4)

Full hands have a cobweb of fine lines, they belong to people who are highly strung and liable to become upset and over-emotional at the drop of a hat. Tense and anxious, people with this type of personality live on their nerves, constantly expecting things to go wrong. Their imagination is so highly developed that they see problems where none exist and try to cross bridges before coming to them. Their nervous and emotional energies are near the surface, they learn about life the hard way. They may distrust their nearest and dearest and blame them for their own weakness.

These hands inflict a degree of sensitivity which makes life an uncomfortable experience. The positive side is creative or artistic talent. If there is also a long head line the subject will be sympathetic and very caring toward others. Unless there is a

strong sun line this person will lack the courage, confidence, tenacity and luck required to carry out his schemes.

The biggest problem is of unnecessary worry. The subject is suspended in a form of mental paralysis between desires and fears; the energies become dissipated and arrive in force as fine worry lines on the hand. These people require a creative outlet in order to avoid becoming frustrated. Routine jobs bore them, they must have variety if they are not to become restless. They hate to be confined but may also be afraid of large spaces and crowds of people. Difficult hands these.

PATCHILY 'FULL' HANDS

If only the mount of Luna is covered in lines, the subject will be nervous of travelling and will only feel comfortable when

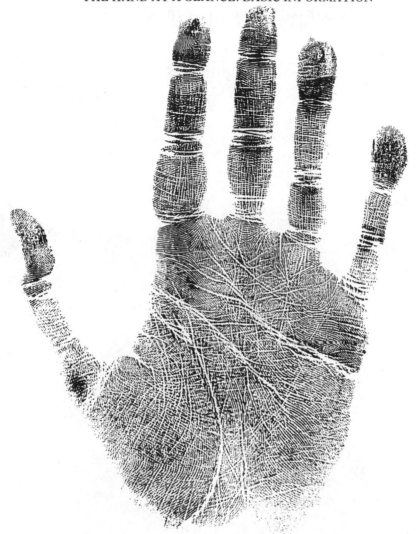

Figure 1.4 Full hand

close to home, where he can keep an eye on his property and family. This type of marking is found on hands that have a characteristic inward dent on the percussion side at the base of the mount of Luna. If the area around the heart line, especially under the area of Saturn, is covered in fine lines, the subject is not at ease in his personal and romantic relationships. If lines extend out onto the palm from inside Venus, there is family aggravation of one kind or another. This may take the form of practical problems or it may indicate an overly critical attitude by a parent or spouse.

HEALTH AND THE FULL HAND

Full hands belong to nervous people who can literally make themselves ill with tension and anxiety. They may suffer from migraine, insomnia or a hundred and one other ailments. However, when the chips are down, these people can sometimes cope better than their calmer 'empty-handed' friends.

The 'Empty' Hand (Fig. 1.5)

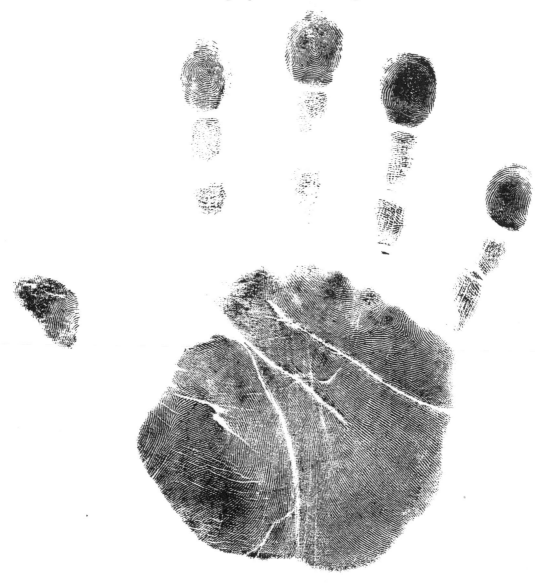

Figure 1.5 Empty hand

The empty hand has few lines on the palmar surface, just the four major lines and one or two others. These people are relatively calm and can cope with most things. They do not worry about other people's opinion of them; they are self-confident, practical and even-tempered. Thinking is logical if rather slow, unimagin-ative unless there is a long sloping head line; the reasoning powers are good being unclouded by emotion. They could be critical at others. If these people have short fingers they would relegate sex to a rather boring weekly routine, romance would not mean much to them. If in addition the head line is straight and fairly short, then the subject would see things in shades of black and white, missing all the subtleties of life.

HEALTH AND THE 'EMPTY' HAND

Because there is no outlet in emotional or neurotic behaviour, these subjects can go down with a terrible bang under severe stress. They may take to drink, smoke and eat too much or just become extremely ill.

CHAPTER TWO

The Hand:

Shapes, Radial and Ulna Sides, Mounts

Hand Shapes

Most people, including us, become defeated by some of the old hand-shape terminology. Who can sort out a philosophic hand from a psychic with the aid of the average palmistry book? Here we have given some descriptions which should match up to reality.

SQUARE HANDS (Fig. 2.1)

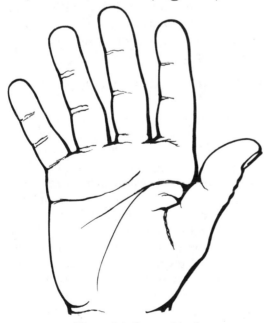

Figure 2.1 Square hand

These hands are of equal width at both the base and the finger ends. They belong to practical, rational people who prefer to live an ordinary life; they like to finish what they start and are not easily bored. We cannot live without these types; they are the 'doers' and they like routines and systems. They usually have only the major lines on the hand and these will be clear cut and fairly straight on a surface which is firm and warm to the touch. There are probably more men with this type of hand than women, but in either sex they are sensible, fairly resourceful and financially sound, good business people and good family folk.

SHORT WIDE HANDS (ELEMENTARY) (Fig. 2.2)

These hands are short and rather squat with square finger ends and a short thumb. The lines are short and straight showing the inability to express feelings. Very elementary hands are found on mentally handicapped people in which case they show an inability to live life to the full; if this is not the case, these people are just rather dense and pedestrian. The short-wide-handed person is best suited to a very basic practical job; he or she does not like

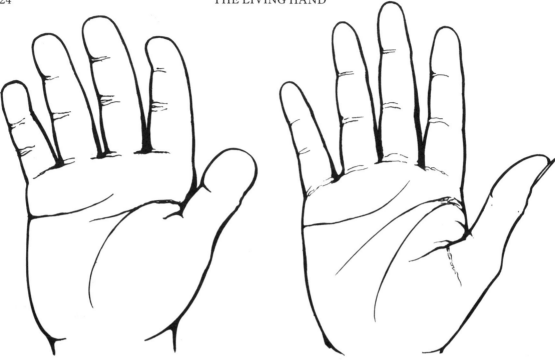

Figure 2.2 Elementary hand   *Figure 2.3* Conic hand

change or new methods and ideas. There is a possibility of a somewhat violent temper as 'elementary' people have difficulty in expressing themselves verbally.

ROUNDED ELEGANT HANDS (CONIC) (Fig. 2.3)

These hands are probably more commonly found on women than men. The shape is gently rounded and rather pleasant to look at. It indicates a fairly gentle, idealistic, sensitive nature with a strong creative streak. Although too energetic to be classed as dreamers, there is a dreamy, romantic side to these people. They need comfort, even a measure of luxury, and have a fairly optimistic outlook. The hand should be fairly firm and springy and the lines gently curving. There could be artistic leanings — these subjects certainly enjoy the results of other people's artistic creations. Warm-hearted people with a liking for peace and family life, they are good at practical tasks as long as they also

have a creative element in them. They are helpful, preferring to follow than to lead, quite resourceful, usually sensible and humorous, but on a bad day can be irritable, unreasonable and oversensitive. Their greatest need is for good personal relationships.

SOFT SQUASHY HANDS (Fig. 2.4)

These people obviously do not do any kind of manual work. They try as much as possible to lead an easy life without having to expend too much physical effort. They can be surprisingly canny in business and it is amazing how frequently this type of hand turns up on a person who has a wide-eyed look of total innocence which hides a surprisingly active mind. They are takers rather than givers. The lines are mainly fine but clearly etched, rather straight and often made up from broken lines (especially the heart line). At best these small soft hands may have pointed fingers which

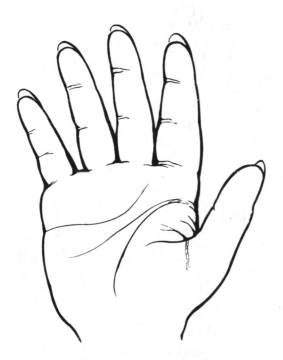
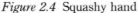

Figure 2.4 Squashy hand

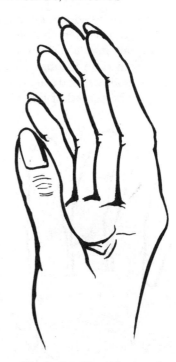

Figure 2.5 Claw-like hand

indicate artistic appreciation and a love of beauty. If the hands are tipped with fat little finger ends and shovel-shaped nails that seem to lift up from the fingers, then beware; these people may look all innocence but they can be *very* manipulative indeed and extremely selfish.

CLAW-LIKE HANDS (Fig. 2.5)

Such hands may indicate a greedy grasping nature, a person who can *only* see his or her own needs and is not prepared to see any other person's point of view. We have seen these hands on clients who are waiting for their partners to die so that they can have the benefit of their goods or money without the bother of having to care for them any longer. The lines may be weak and sloppy or quite strongly etched, but the mounts are rather flat (with the possible exception of Jupiter) and the whole hand is cramped in appearance with a large hollow in the middle. The nails are likely to be long and narrow, and if they also curve like claws,

there is an extremely selfish, greedy or grasping personality. The skin surface often has a crumpled appearance and if the palmist gently makes a dent in the surface when the hand is relaxed, the dent will stay there until the hand is stretched and used once more! These people rarely go out to work as they are not interested in either a career for themselves or, heaven forbid, helping others in any way. If they do have to work, they make life a misery for all their colleagues as they are only in it for what they can get and have no time for the social niceties.

A-SHAPED (SPATULATE) HANDS (Fig. 2.6)

A-shaped hands are narrow at the base and wider at the finger ends. This is an independent energetic type who has an original way of looking at life. He or she must have a physical or sporting outlet, but most of all the A-shape type needs mental challenges and problems to get his or her teeth into. He or she could be a craftsman, inventor or even writer, but he or she enjoys going out into the open air, or out onto water from time to time. These subjects could be good around the farm as they are unlikely to be scared of large animals.

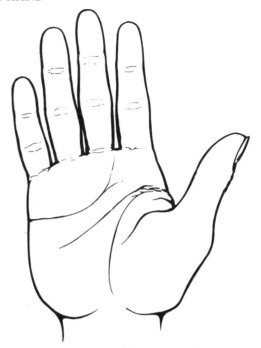

Figure 2.7 V-shaped hand

KNOTTY OR KNOBBLY HANDS (PHILOSOPHIC) (Fig. 2.8)

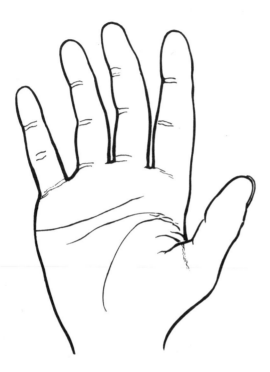

Figure 2.6 A-shaped hand

V-SHAPED (SPATULATE) HANDS (Fig. 2.7)

This subject is also inventive, but could be less of a craftsman. Either type of spatulate subject will be highly ambitious and from time to time adopt an abrupt and hasty manner towards slower people who get in the way. There is a great need for physical activity, as they find it hard to sit still and want to make the most of every opportunity in life. They enjoy a challenge, and need an outlet in vigorous sports — this is the successful tennis or squash player. These highly-strung, energetic types would make enthusiastic practical scientists, geographers or explorers.

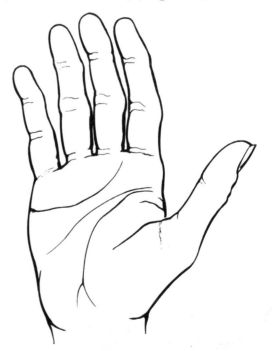

Figure 2.8 Knotty or knobbly hand

These hands turn up on intellectual types who live in the realm of ideas. They are pleasant, good company and very interesting to talk with; they appreciate creativity. They enjoy the company of their family, but neither sex is terribly practical around the home. They can be easily sidetracked by an interesting discussion, a good book or a fascinating word game with the children. Those readers who are keen on astrology might see these people as being Aquarian types. The lines on these hands are usually well formed, gently curving but not too deeply etched.

LONG NARROW HANDS (Fig. 2.9)

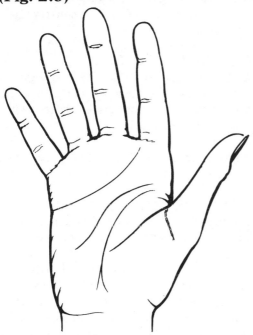

Figure 2.9 Long narrow hand

These people lack balance and common sense. They may be terribly clever artistically but their rather inward-looking, self-centred nature makes it difficult for them to relate comfortably to others. They lack practicality and are probably better off working quietly at home. They find other people rather hard to cope with at times.

They do not have much physical strength or stamina — this is obvious from the rather thin and reedy lines. If there is a network of very fine lines, they will be oversensitive and nervy. They may fancy themselves and put on airs and graces.

LONG DELICATE HANDS (PSYCHIC) (Fig. 2.10)

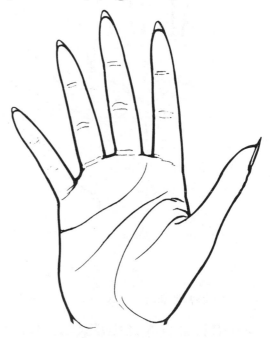

Figure 2.10 Long delicate hand (psychic)

These hands have slim tapering fingers, a straight thinnish thumb and smooth-looking fingers. These people are sensitive and imaginative, possibly artistic too. Their feelings are very near the surface; they can be easily hurt and can identify with other people's suffering. There is a tendency to overdramatize themselves and play the martyr until something comes along to distract their attention. They fall deeply in love, and may suffer from unrequited love, because they are shy about revealing their feelings; they are embarrassed about sexual matters. They will suffer disappointments in life because their standards are unrealistically high.

MONKEY-LIKE HANDS
(Fig. 2.11)

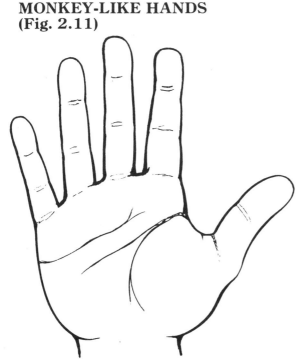

Figure 2.11 Monkey-like hand

Such hands have slim, graspy fingers. These people are talented, quick, clever and somewhat slippery and untrustworthy.

SHORT, PLUMP ENERGETIC HANDS

There is a certain type of small hand which is sometimes rather 'full' but not soft to the touch. These people are kindly, energetic and rather proud. They make good spouses but, possibly, rather impatient parents. The lines on these hands tend to curve, the fullish mounts show warmth of character but the characteristically small A-shaped (spatulate) fingernails — a rather bluey-mauve in colour — point to a good deal of personal ambition.

SQUARE SLIM HANDS

These hands have slightly tapering fingers.

These folk are practical, decisive, energetic, honest, straightforward and good natured. They do not like to let anyone down. Living with this type means being prepared for an energetic relationship, sharing in his or her ideas and enthusiasms.

SHORT WIDE HANDS

These have fingers that taper towards the tips. The thumb may bend a long way back and curve outwards. Practical and realistic but with a really terrific sense of humour, this type will place a high value on humour in friends of either sex. They are creative, generous and helpful, also good with their hands. They are very sociable and put this to good use when trying to form relationships.

A LARGE THUMB

A large thumb could be either straight or bent, giving the hand a lopsided look. Ambitious and competitive, these people tackle life energetically, whether it be work, hobbies or school exams. They are so single-minded that they usually get what they want.

MIXED HANDS

Some hands defy categorization — they might be a mixture of any of the types which we have already mentioned, or they may be in a class of their own. Basically, if the radial side is more developed, then the subject will be energetic in worldly matters; if the ulna side is stronger, more home-loving and imaginative. A square palm with long fingers indicates a practical artist — illustrator, dressmaker etc; a long square palm with short conic fingers, a quick thinking and acting person who despite appearances has the application to finish what he or she starts and make a good job of it.

Radial/Ulna Sides of the Hand

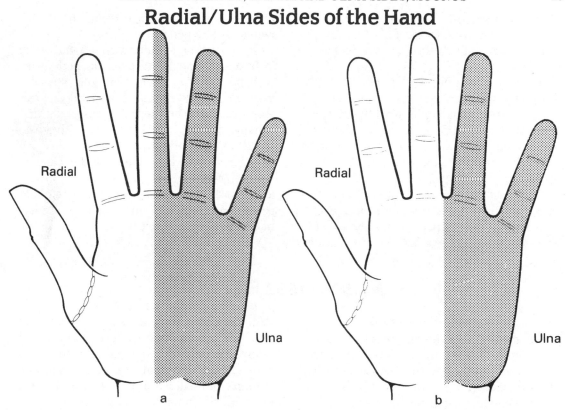

Figure 2.12 Radial and Ulna

RADIAL (Fig. 2.12)

This is the thumb side of the hand and it is concerned with the outer personality. It could be termed masculine or active, and if well developed shows that the subject copes well with worldly affairs. A well-developed radial side would make for someone who is practical, businesslike, possibly executive material. He would cope well with any situation which requires assertion, confidence and a sense of personal authority. The subject will be sexually active, possibly rather demanding and will have a strong desire to live life to the full.

ULNA

This is the percussion side of the hand and it is concerned with the inner personality — feminine, intuitive, receptive. If this side is well developed, the subject is highly imaginative and may use this imagination

as part of his work or to enrich his life. This person will be understanding toward others — gentle, caring and pleasant — will get on well with children and animals, and have a love of art, music and all creative work.

THE IMPORTANCE OF BALANCE

In palmistry, everything depends on balance. Too much of one aspect on a hand will cause that person to be overdeveloped in one area of life and lacking in some of the others. If a hand appears to be lopsided, then we suggest that you take a piece of paper and cover up half of the hand and see what you would have if the missing half

---

NB Some people divide the hand into radial and ulna by running a line down the middle of the Saturn finger (a). We prefer to leave the Saturn finger in one piece and to take the line down *between* Saturn and Apollo (b).

looked the same as the half you can still see; then change halves. This can give a quite astonishing picture of two people in one.

If the radial side is far heavier, the subject will be active, competitive, materialistic, capable in worldly matters but could find difficulty in expressing or understanding feelings. Mystically or astro-logically speaking, this would be a 'young spirit', an Aries type.

Too much ulna is rare — it is usually the other way round — but when it does occur — it would imply a personality awash with emotion and imagination, longing to be creative but lacking the drive to do so. This would be a super mystical Pisces type.

Obviously the subject with a hand which is balanced and fairly even on both sides will not have either trait too strongly marked. If the hand is generally weak looking, then neither the assertive and capable nor the creative and sensitive side will be developed; a kind of peevish selfishness will take over. If the hand is generally strong and firm then the person-ality has a nice balance between action and reception, creativity and scientific ability, understanding and action.

Mounts (see Fig. 1.1)

Perhaps we should think of the mounts as the names of countries and seas that appear on a map. They may not have too much importance in themselves, but each one has its own character and this must be borne in mind when looking at the lines which touch them and the marks which appear on them. They are *all* called mounts, even Neptune and Saturn which often look more like valleys. The mounts of Jupiter, Saturn, Apollo and Mercury are the energy reserves of the fingers.

THE RADIAL MOUNTS

JUPITER
This represents the practical use of one's will power, ambition and pride. If well developed it confers executive ability, strong personal beliefs, even religious beliefs, plus the desire for and ability to use authority. If overdeveloped the person would be arrogant, overambitious, selfish, a bully or a bigot. If underdeveloped there is not much ambition or personal dignity plus a dislike of authority.

VENUS
This represents love, both the type of affection one has for family and friends and, to some extent, sexual love; also personal values, energy and stamina and enjoyment of life. If full and firm the subject will have plenty of energy and stamina and will live life to the full. He will enjoy music, dancing, beauty and the arts, a good meal and a night out. He will probably have a good sense of humour. If the mount is full but soft, this can indicate a person who is self-indulgent, lazy and greedy. A cramped small mount signifies a person who, apart from lacking in physical stamina, would be cold and overconcerned with the practicalities of life to the exclusion of enjoyment. This type could be selfish, unsympathetic, mean, unloving and in an odd way, domineering.

LOWER MARS
It might help the reader to think of lower Mars as being the attacking force, upper Mars being tenacity in defence. We some-times see a really high lower Mars on military hands, also on those who have made a hobby out of scouting or some such paramilitary organization. If fairly large, the subject is assertive, capable, something of a go-getter. If almost missing, he would sit and whinge rather than go out and do something to change his situation.

THE BALANCE MOUNTS

These are neither radial nor ulna; they hold the balance between the inner and outer sides of the personality.

SATURN

This mount is concerned with practical ambitions, earned money, serious thought, scientific investigation, solitude, practical gains but emotional limitations. If large or obvious, there could be a gloomy, pessimistic, solitary attitude to life — the subject would be cautious or easily depressed.

NEPTUNE

This is the bridge between Venus and Luna — or, in other terms, the conscious and the unconscious drives. If the mount is equal in height with Venus and Luna, the subject is sympathetic to others and able to key into feelings, both his own and someone else's. He can translate ideas into reality, like a painter or musician who dreams up an idea and brings it to life, or a writer who takes obscure ideas and expresses them in a coherent manner. There are also important health matters which appear on or near this part of the hand (see Chapter 12).

THE ULNA MOUNTS

APOLLO

If well developed, this mount indicates charm, good manners, creativity, a liking for children and animals, sports, arts and hobbies; if overdeveloped, greed, extravagance, vanity — could be a gambler.

MERCURY

This mount is concerned with self-expression, communications, business, machinery, money, literary and scientific matters, health and relationships. If overdeveloped, the subject could be a cunning confidence trickster. If underdeveloped, painfully shy, unable to express himself, with no business acumen.

LUNA (Fig. 2.13)

This relates to the unconscious, the imagination, creativity, travel, also a love of the sea and a need for freedom. If well developed, there could be a liking for gentle outdoor sports and pursuits, especially fishing.

A high mount of Luna is supposed to show linguistic ability, but we feel a love of travel is just as likely.

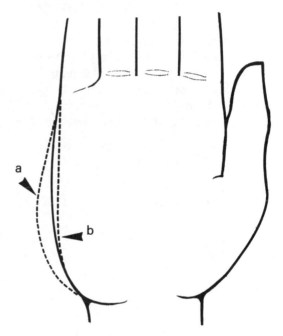

Figure 2.13 A bulge at the Percussion edge

PLUTO (BETWEEN LUNA AND THE WRIST)

If this mount is developed there will be a restless quality, a need to get away from time to time, plus the ability to translate theoretical ideas into practice.

UPPER MARS (Fig. 2.13)

Tenacity, courage, aggression. If fairly full and thick at the percussion edge, the subject will be able to cope with a crisis and also stand up for himself. If this is exceptionally prominent, high, full and stands upwards and outwards from the hand at the percussion edge (a), the subject may be argumentative, possibly in extreme cases with a violent temper.

Here are a couple of ideas about this mount which were given to us by our friend, John Lindsay. Firstly, a thick mount gives calm acceptance and resilience to shock and surprise, whereas a thin one leaves the subject flabbergasted at sudden surprising events; and secondly, a mount which curves outwards at the percussion on both Mars and Luna is a sign of creativity. This person would find his own method of doing things. If the edge is straight (b), the subject is good at interpreting the ideas of others — possibly also good at linking in to the thoughts of others in order to make sense of them. The first person would be able to work out original ideas whereas the second could carry them out for him.

If the head line goes into the upper Mars area, the subject would be a very convincing salesman and could sell refrigerators to Eskimos!

PLAIN OF MARS (see Fig. 1.1)

This is the centre of the hand. It has no specific character of its own but it is the area where the lines cross, influence and activate one another.

A thin mount of Mars shows a low level of energy and resistance to disease. V line formations on the Mount of Apollo would back up this theory by showing some form of disablement. (See Fig. 8.1p)

CHAPTER THREE

Fingers and Phalanges

Fingers

LENGTH OF FINGERS

Average fingers are about three-quarters to seven-eighths the length of the palm, short fingers are less than three-quarters and long fingers are the same length or longer than the palm. Long-fingered people have patience with detail but find it hard to motivate themselves — they find large-scale projects off-putting. Short-fingered people are starters, not runners; they have initiative and can conceive grand plans but they are quickly bored with detailed work and daily chores. It is interesting to note that people who have somewhat stubby fat fingers often love music but never have the patience to master an instrument. Long-fingered people have talent and patience but often lack the energy and initiative to cash in on their gifts. On a normal hand, the Saturn (medius or middle) finger is the longest, with either the Jupiter (index) or Apollo (ring) finger coming next, and the Mercury (little) finger being the shortest.

THROUGH THICK AND THIN

Thick-fingered people do not like to waste time — they jump straight into a situation and get on with it (especially if the fingers are short). They may live or work in a mess because they prefer to be doing something purposeful rather than spend time clearing up. Their minds work quickly, they focus intuitively on a problem to produce the ideal solution. They are direct and honest, but tactless. They do not set out to hurt other people's feelings, it is just that they do not stop to think sometimes and they lack patience with those whom they consider to be fools. These subjects have more than a dash of the zodiac sign of Aries about them.

Thin-fingered people are more precise in their thinking. They need to take time about a task and tackle it in a logical manner. They are thoughtful, diplomatic and patient.

KNUCKLES

Knobbly knuckles are a feature of rather cautious people who choose to play it safe. They may moan and groan on occasion about their situation but will put up with the status quo rather than face change.

KNOTS OF MENTAL ORDER

Knotty first knuckles (near the finger tips) suggest a methodical mind, good at logic or research, but not given to flashes of intuition.

KNOTS OF MATERIAL ORDER

Knots on the second knuckles (middle of the fingers) suggest a person who works in an orderly fashion, again logical but not as hidebound as the subject with knots on both sets of knuckles. (See Fig. 3.26)

HOW THE FINGERS ARE 'SET' (see Fig. 3.2)

The junction where the fingers join the hands varies from one person to another. We refer to this base level of the fingers as the 'setting'. Some people have a gentle curve where their fingers join their palm, others have a straight line. The setting of the fingers may disguise their true length by making one finger appear shorter than the others. The easiest way to measure the *exact* length of each finger is to take a bit of ribbon and a felt-tipped pen and mark off each finger against the ribbon (see Fig. 3.1). Fingers which are set in line suggest a rigid, ambitious personality, a gentle curve would be a balanced personality, and a very sharp V formation, someone who has a giant sense of inadequacy.

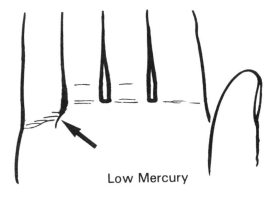

Low Mercury

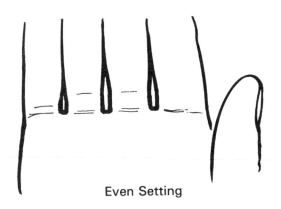

Even Setting

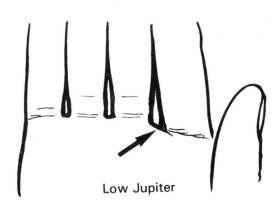

Low Jupiter

Figure 3.2 Settings

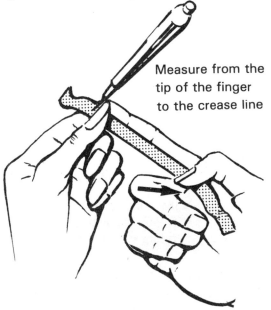

Measure from the tip of the finger to the crease line

Figure 3.1 Measuring fingers

THE JUPITER (INDEX) FINGER

LONG JUPITER FINGER

These people like to have their own way

and need to stamp their personality on their surroundings. They are unable to sacrifice their independence for the sake of others. They tend to have strong, highly personal, religious or philosophical views. They are ambitious, hard to dominate, influence or change. The ego is well developed and the personality may run from sociable and well adjusted to pompous, self-important or just plain selfish. They are very interested in money because of the power and the security it represents and they will go all out to find and keep it. They may hoard it or spend it depending on other factors on the hand, but they must have access to it.

SHORT JUPITER FINGER

People with short Jupiter fingers lack a sense of conviction. Lacking confidence in themselves, they may not have a clear idea of their direction in life, or even of their own identity. They tend to measure themselves by other people's standards and can lose heart when criticized — they need reassurance from others. These people can be fairly easily manipulated and are willing to sacrifice their own desires for the needs of others. Often very loving and caring, they must make sure that they do leave time for themselves to pursue their own interests. It would help them if they could learn to rely on their own judgement.

Sometimes a long Apollo finger can make the Jupiter finger *seem* short, also a low-set Jupiter will look shorter than it is (see Fig. 3.2). If the Jupiter finger is shorter than the Apollo finger, the subject may have a personality which is perfectly well adjusted but he will be more interested in expressing his creativity than in making (and holding on to) a lot of money.

HIGH-SET JUPITER

This indicates self-confidence and ambition. If the finger is also long and carries a whorl pattern on the finger print, there is very little which would stop this person from achieving his aims in life.

LEVEL-SET JUPITER

This shows a balanced attitude. This subject is neither overambitious, egotistical, timid nor retiring. He is helpful and understanding up to a point; he likes to make his own decisions but will co-operate and discuss these where appropriate.

LOW-SET JUPITER

This setting represents quite a problem as the subject is very unsure of himself. He has little courage or ability to stand up for himself. He may be extremely shy, especially if there is an arch formation on the Jupiter finger print. He prefers others to make decisions, he fits in with other people's plans and does not like to speak out even on his own behalf. There could be a tendency to self-sacrifice or martydom.

DISCREPANCIES IN THE JUPITER FINGERS ON THE RIGHT AND LEFT HAND

This shows that the person has changed himself due to circumstances. If the minor hand has the longer Jupiter finger, then the subject's personality has been squashed in some way by the demands of other people. If the dominant hand has the longer Jupiter finger — a much more common feature — then the subject has learned how to express his personality and to exert his will power. He has made himself fight for his rightful share of a place in the sun.

THE SATURN (MIDDLE, MEDIUS) FINGER

This finger is associatied with the everyday practicalities and problems of earning a living. It is usually the longest finger on the hand and may sit squarely on a line with Jupiter, Apollo or both. Most people have squarish or slightly conic finger ends and nails on the Saturn finger. It is associated with farming, property, land and investments, also the ability to study, scientific aptitudes and the gloomier aspects of religious or philosophical thought. It marks the balance between the radial and ulna sides of the hand and shows how the conscious and unconscious sides of the subject's nature blend together.

LONG SATURN FINGER

This is often found in serious people with the ability to study hard and concentrate on a project; this is especially so if the head line travels straight across the hand aiming directly for the percussion edge. If the finger is exceptionally long, the subject will be pessimistic, easily downhearted, even morbid. If a number of fine lines suddenly appear on the mount of Saturn, the subject would be going through a period of depression. A reasonably long Saturn finger endows good organizational skills and an instinctive understanding of economics. This person will be materialistic, especially if the third phalange is full and fat. If the hands are either square or clawlike, this subject will never take any kind of risk. The combination of long Jupiter and Saturn fingers point to strong religious views with a blinkered and inflexible attitude, especially if the fingers are stiff and unbending.

A reasonably long Saturn finger shows that the subject is interested in stability, both emotional and financial. There will be a sensible attitude to saving — this person would take out a mortgage and then take good care of the property. There will be a love of the countryside and an interest in ecology — the preservation and protection of our planet. Astrologically speaking, this finger carries some of the attributes of Taurus and Capricorn.

SHORT SATURN FINGER

This person is venturesome, will take a chance on life and in business. If the Apollo finger is rather long and stays close to the Saturn finger, then there will be an instinct for gambling and risk taking. If the Jupiter finger is the closest in length and proximity to Saturn, then the subject will be rather egotistical and may not really consider the possibility of failure. Popular and successful showbusiness personalities tend to have Saturn, Apollo and even Jupiter fingers all of more or less the same length. These people may be untidy, scatty, disorganized or compulsive gamblers, but if the Saturn finger is not too short, they will display great zest for life and the ability to back a hunch and win. They are not so good at conserving their winnings and need a partner with longer Saturn fingers to help them save sensibly.

SETTING AND THE SATURN FINGER

This finger is nearly always set either on a level with the adjoining fingers or perhaps a little higher. In the rare case of a subject with a low-set Saturn finger, he would be unable to cope with daily life, and would lack balance between the conscious and unconscious mind leading to very inconsistent behaviour. He or she could be aggressive, violent, even psychotic.

THE APOLLO (RING) FINGER

This finger is associated with the more enjoyable aspects of life such as creativity, also the inclination to take chances in life; these may range from slight risks to out and out gambles. The Apollo finger deals with the fatalistic dreamy side of life and could give success of a glamorous kind if there are other harder features showing on the hand, such as a longish Saturn finger and a strongly-formed head line and/or fate line. It is also connected with the home and family and a love of children.

LONG APOLLO FINGER

Be careful with determining the actual length of the fingers here as they may be disguised by the setting on the hand (see page 34).

These subjects have pleasant manners and a nice appearance. They like good clothes and need attractive surroundings. They are broad-minded, generous, less likely to live by the book than others, less inhibited than most. They may be scatty, not quite of this world and too ready to put their week's wages on the head of some spavined nag, but they are fun. Self-expression is more important than financial gain. This subject may be artistic and musical, especially if the first phalange splays outwards, or a clever craftsman if the first phalange carries a droplet. The natural dreaminess may not be too notice-able to others if all the fingers are fairly short, the thumb is strong and the head line not too curved. These people are fond of children and enjoy homelife as long as the atmosphere at home is pleasant and easy-going. They will make sacrifices for the family and would always prefer to live in harmony rather than fight for their rights. They can be quite ambitious with regard to their creative interests, especially if the Jupiter finger leans toward Saturn.

SHORT APOLLO FINGER

This subject is ambitious, self-motivated and not about to make sacrifices on behalf of others; capable and practical, he is not usually given to fits of dreamy irresponsi-bility. If the head line and life line are 'tied' where they start on the hands, he will seek security, and will want guarantees wherever possible. He may either be some-what narrow-minded or will just tend to see things his own way. If there is a long Mercury finger, this person could be a good public speaker but rather a misery in private life. He is responsible, reliable and decent, if rather boring. He would not be an inventive lover.

SETTING AND THE APOLLO FINGER

When set in line with Saturn, there is an air of confidence and optimism, any creativity will be of a practical nature. If it is set significantly lower than the Saturn finger the subject is not so imaginative and may despise anything which does not have a practical use.

THE MERCURY FINGER

This finger really is the most difficult to understand as it is on the ulna (instinctive) side of the hand and is concerned with how we express ourselves. It shows how we go about getting what we need by day-to-day co-operation and interaction with others.

This finger shows how we communicate, whether we are fluent talkers, good writers or have the ability to sort out ideas and images logically. Are we truthful or sneaky fibbers? Do we need the excitement and challenge of a career in sales or finance or do we just prefer to plod along in a steadily familiar job? Even sexual communication is shown on this finger.

LONG MERCURY FINGER

Setting can make this finger look short when in fact it is not. The long Mercury finger belongs to a subject who can express himself well. If the Saturn finger is also long and he has a long straight head line with a fairly firmly marked fate line he will have a scientific mind. The mind will be imaginative and creative if the Apollo finger is long, there is a slope to the head line and a well-defined Apollo line. These people have broad minds as they want to know what is going on in the world. They are sociable and learn from chatting to others; they also make good students and teachers as they cannot resist the oppor-tunity of communicating and spreading knowledge. They may be wordy, verbose and possibly boring when on their favourite soap box, unless there is a little loop of humour on the hand between the mounts of Mercury and Apollo. There are drawn towards intelligent and interesting people. Anybody who needs to influence others, be it politically, in business, in the fields of science, education, literature or art, will need at least a reasonably long Mercury with a long first and second phalange (see pages 40 and 45). This is also true for negotiators and business people who need to confer with or organize others.

A slight curve in this finger shows both business sense and a sensible attitude to money. This subject has a fairly firm attitude with the ability to stick to his guns and finish what he starts. Too great a curve indicates obstinacy.

There is something to be gleaned from the Mercury finger about the subject's attitude to sex. If the finger is long and straight he might be a bit of a 'chaser', if curved, then more of a family man and rather choosy about whom he marries; a little 'step' on the inside of the third phalange shows sexuality.

SHORT MERCURY FINGER

This is an indication of intense shyness. This subject will take a long time to gain the confidence and maturity to go 'a-courting' especially if the moons are wholly or partly missing from all the fingernails. There is a hatred of public speaking or of being centre stage for any reason. This does not mean that the subject has a poor opinion of himself — on the contrary, he may have quite a large ego — but he just hates to be exposed or placed in the limelight. He is easily embarrassed and soon becomes tongue-tied. He prefers to lead a quiet life, be a backroom boy rather than a front runner.

One kind of subject with a short Mercury finger would be the type of 'little man' who attaches himself to a large and overpowering woman — the seaside postcard type of set-up; this man may in fact be quite obstinate and awkward to live with — after all he is, in essence, afraid of life, narrow-minded. He does not read much except for the newspaper, he is a creature of habit and safety. He lives a rich life at second hand through his lady wife! Get the picture? He may have strange secret sexual desires but would run a mile if he had to 'perform' in any way.

EXCEPTIONALLY SHORT MERCURY FINGER

This shows some kind of sexual peculiarity. This person may have a severe lack of confidence, due to being unusually tall, short, fat, thin etc. The subject could have a nice appearance but *feel* him or herself to be unattractive. They find it difficult to express themselves sexually and hard to keep the attention of the opposite sex. This is also sometimes a sign of mental handicap.

SETTING AND THE MERCURY FINGER

The Mercury finger can be set either in line with the other fingers or lower. If set in line, the personality will be fairly outgoing and businesslike; if low set there is talent but this will be brought out in private through work and study at home. These people have a creative imagination and may be writers or artists. They dream a little too much, especially if there is a very sloping head line. There could be a tendency toward self-deception and daydreaming, if the subjects have a long sloping head line and a high mount of Neptune, but this may be a necessary part of their creative mentality.

We have seen books mention that people with bent and twisted Mercury fingers are liars and criminals, but often this is a family peculiarity, rather like clubbed thumbs and not necessarily the sign of a candidate for a wanted poster!

INCLINING OR LATERAL CURVING FINGERS (Fig. 3.3)

The way fingers curve and lean toward each other is important. Ask your subject to hold his hands upright, better still, take a print of his hand. Look at the finger tips; if they lean naturally toward any of the other fingers this will show where the flow of energy is inhibited and has become dependent upon the energy of the finger it leans upon. This leaning must be natural and not due to disease of malformation. If one finger is slightly tucked behind another, think of the energies attached to those fingers and apply a little logic. For instance, the Apollo finger tucked under the Saturn finger on the dominant hand would imply that the subject was having his

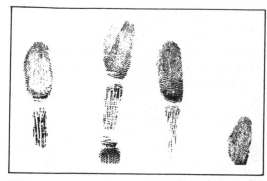

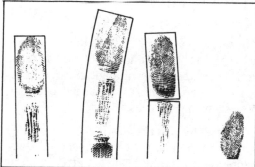

Figure 3.3 Inclination

or her creativity stifled by a regimented routine or limiting circumstances.

If the top phalange is bent, the mental faculties will be inhibited, making the subject a slow thinker. There might be mental depression too. Fig. 3.3 shows the Jupiter finger straight and the Saturn finger curved with the Apollo finger positively *bent*.

JUPITER FINGER CURVED TOWARD THE THUMB
This gives a materialistic outlook on life and a dynamic purposeful personality, also a need for personal freedom, an independent nature, especially if there is a fair sized gap between the Jupiter and Saturn fingers.

JUPITER FINGER CURVED TOWARD SATURN
Self-assertion, an attitude of a positive, persistent working towards one's aims and intentions, this subject sets out to get what he wants. Inclined to be emotionally secretive, he finds it hard to unwind and reveal his true self. He may *appear* to be open and chatty and full of interesting anecdotes, but will be very careful not to say anything personally revealing.

SATURN FINGER CURVED TOWARD JUPITER
A serious type of person, who is emotionally rather inhibited. He may look outwards for happiness, by seeking recognition in sports or some other kind of achievement. Restless and ambitious.

JUPITER AND SATURN BOTH CURVED TOWARDS APOLLO AND MERCURY
A need for inner understanding. If the life line curves around the lower Venus these people are not looking for a career but some sort of inner understanding and fulfilment.

SATURN CURVED TOWARD APOLLO
This person is pressurized by family, domestic demands and duties which may conflict with the career. The subject could be searching for self-expression and a feeling of achievement and job satisfaction, not necessarily for more money.

There is an old wives' tale that if the top phalange of Saturn slews sideways toward Apollo, the subject will one day write for a living. We do not know whether this is true or not but Sasha's finger has this kink in it!

APOLLO CURVED TOWARD SATURN
These people get no pleasure from domestic responsibilities, they find housework boring. They prefer to be professional people. You can check your findings by looking at the life line (Chapter 7). Emotional, intuitive, intellectual and rational, they may have an inferiority complex about sex!

If the top phalange bends toward Saturn, this may give a mediumistic quality.

MERCURY FINGER CURVED TOWARD APOLLO
This person can help people by talking, listening and consoling those who are

unhappy. If the curve is extreme, they are shrewd in business, rather good salesmen so long as they believe in their product. They have an optimistic nature but may be rather defensive; they make up their own minds.

MERCURY FINGER CURVING OUTWARDS

Unsure of themselves, these subjects need someone reliable to give them backing and encouragement. They prefer to blend in with the environment and not to press their own opinion on others.

Phalanges

Each finger is divided into three phalanges. The first phalange shows how we think, the second shows how we apply that thinking and the third shows how we act — even if we act without thinking.

Thick phalanges show a coarse side to the nature whilst slender phalanges show refinement and delicacy. At the same time, one must bear in mind that thicker phalanges show energy and enterprise while the slim phalanges show a weaker, more nervous attitude.

THE FIRST PHALANGE

This includes the finger prints and finger nails. Finger tips, like toes, are the extremities of the body; they are the first to shrivel and die if the body is under severe attack through illness or frostbite; they give the palmist the first impression of the subject and his nature. They show how the subject views the world about him and the influence he has upon it.

LONG FIRST PHALANGES

Intuitive, studious, orderly; the outlook is philosophical and religious rather than materialistic. These people delight in mental activities such as debating, reading and crossword puzzles, they enjoy new ideas and can be very entertaining.

SHORT FIRST PHALANGES

Materialistic, possibly practical, suspicious of people, these subjects only understand tangibles and have little sense of faith or inspiration. They are mentally lazy, not inclined to study or grasp new concepts.

FINGER TIPS

ROUND TIPS (Fig 3.4)

These people do not like friction — they seek beauty, truth and might be too trusting. They are open minded, creative; they make clever, shrewd, fairly cautious, honest business types.

POINTED TIPS (Fig. 3.5)

Pin-sharp minds, quick intellect — these people go to the heart of a matter, sum up the situation quickly but cannot see the overall picture. They react instinctively to people and immediately form likes and dislikes. Once these opinions are formed they are uncompromising which makes it difficult for them to act diplomatically or to see behind someone else's outer manner or find excuses for the behaviour or attitude of those they do not take to. They have good organizational and delegation skills but cannot cope with too many details.

Very pointed finger tips belong to the beautiful dreamer. These people are cautious, discreet and have a mental ideal of the kind of life which would best suit themselves. They are frequently very good looking, they pay attention to their appearance and are personally fussy. They can be a source of inspiration to others but lack the energy to do much for themselves; they certainly will not set out to do anything for others.

A-SHAPED, SPATULATE TIPS (Fig. 3.6)

Outgoing, outdoor types — independent people with restless minds, they can see the whole picture and bring all the component parts together and therefore make good scientists, lawyers, also good performers, sportsmen. They like to bring the fruits of their hands and brains together, and may be inventive craftsmen and engineers.

SQUARE TIPS (Fig. 3.7)
Down-to-earth types, blunt manner, slow

minds. They are conformists and can be dogmatic, conservative. They like to see justice done. If the phalanges are long, they make good lawyers, bankers, clerks, counsellors. They are good with documents, especially the small print.

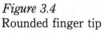
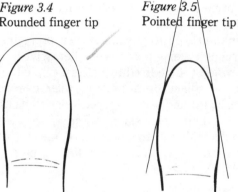

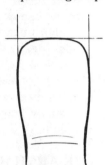

Figure 3.4
Rounded finger tip

Figure 3.5
Pointed finger tip

Figure 3.6
Spatulate finger tip

Figure 3.7
Square finger tip

SIDE VIEW OF FIRST PHALANGE

TAPERING (Fig. 3.8)
These people put their minds to good use but lack physical stamina. They are imaginative, affectionate, spiritual rather than materialistic in outlook.

COARSE HEAVY TIPS (Fig. 3.9)
These people are down to earth, materialistic, sensual and self-indulgent, sometimes coarse in behaviour. If the phalange is

short, they could be unimaginative plodders; if long, quite sharp in business, capable, not likely to be beaten in an argument.

BULGY TIP, DROPLETS (Fig. 3.10)
Much more refined than the coarse-tipped type, they have a highly developed sense of touch. Amazingly dextrous, they rarely drop anything (good jugglers maybe)! They are sensitive, intellectual with creative gifts, particularly for anything that de-

Figure 3.8 Tapering finger tip   *Figure 3.9* Coarse finger tip   *Figure 3.10* Bulgy finger tip

mands a sense of 'feel' such as dress-making, gardening, sculpture, playing a musical instrument, even more so if there is a prominent droplet on Apollo. Their natures can be rather intense and one must look at the head line to see if it slopes to Luna, indicating a sensitive mind.

Finger Prints

Finger prints are formed before birth and are an unchanging inherited characteristic. Each person's prints are unique. Finger-print patterns must be read bearing in mind the shape of the hand, the fingers, thumb and the head line, as the other parts of the hand will show how the subject deals with the inborn characteristics locked up in the prints. Ideally each print pattern should be in, or just below, the centre of the first phalange of each finger. It is possible to find hands that carry only one type of print — usually loops or whorls — but most people have a mixture of prints.

inward looking, secretive and self-defensive; there may have been unhappiness and unpleasant events early in life. Subjects who have more than just a couple of arches need to be encouraged to be a little more trusting, more outgoing and to think more positively about their problems. Although very unsure of themselves, if they do become fired by enthusiasm, either for a project or a person, they can go overboard and bore everyone else to death with their obsession. They are not intellectual but that does not mean that they cannot appreciate the finer things in life.

THE ARCH (Fig. 3.11)

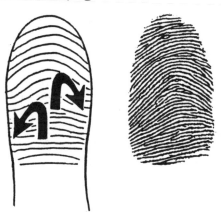

Figure 3.11
The arch finger print

COMPOSITE WHORL OR DOUBLE LOOP (Fig. 3.12)

Figure 3.12
The composite whorl
finger print

This is shaped like a humped-back bridge, it deflects energy back down the finger. It represents the simplest type of personality — practical, shy and rather ordinary. If there are many suppression lines below the arch (see page 45), this will add tension and neurosis to the personality. Arches do not bestow an easy life, everything has to be worked for. The personality is withdrawn,

This looks like a side view of two hands which are interlocked. The energy of the whorl goes into the centre where the two forces meet. This leads to duality, indecision, the ability to see both sides of an argument or the possibilities of two courses of action. We have noticed that psychic people seem to have this formation on their thumbs or their Jupiter fingers.

A double loop on the Mercury finger may show bisexuality.

THE WHORL (Fig. 3.13)

Figure 3.13
The whorl finger print

This looks like a whirlpool with the energy running smoothly into the centre. These types are self-centred and orientated towards the inner realms of thought, individualism and independence. These people's strong reserves of inner strength and determination cause them to set their own standards and carve their own path through life. If there are many whorls on the fingers (and especially on the Jupiter finger) this subject will be hard working and very successful — doors will open for him. Cool, calculating and emotionally controlled, this is the anti-hero type — Al Pacino in *The Godfather*, the young Sean Connery as Bond. This person would do well in the armed services where his highly-tuned and carefully-focused intellect would take him to the top. Although rarely emotionally vulnerable, such types may wonder why they do not get too much out of relationships, and will need a compliant marriage partner who is either content to remain in the background or who has a separate career and interests.

WHORLS

(a) WHORL ON JUPITER
A blinkered attitude, unable to see other points of view or understand other people's way of life; probably not that interested in other people anyway. Pays great attention to career, focuses on career direction without being distracted by other, potentially competing issues.

(b) WHORL ON SATURN
Could be too serious, even depressive, lonely character, self-disciplined, successful in a highly original way, ambitious and obstinate with an air of importance and a touch-me-not attitude. The marriage partner will be chosen for suitability.

(c) WHORL ON APOLLO
Artistic ability, sets emotional standards, considers himself entitled to dictate the partner's behaviour and feelings. Personal tastes are set early in life and are hard to change.

(d) WHORL ON MERCURY
Teaching ability, wants to expand mental horizons, research, reach for answers. Journalists, broadcasters, seekers after truth; this subject is determined, successful but shy and unsure of himself emotionally.

LOOP (Fig. 3.14)

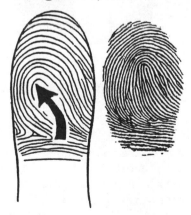

Figure 3.14
The loop finger print

This is the most commonly-found pattern in which the energy is deflected to one side or the other. The loops *usually* enter the fingers from the ulna side with the occasional radial loop on the Jupiter finger. This person is friendly, adaptable and responsive to people; a good team worker who needs variety both in working and social life. The mind is lively, elastic, quick and humorous. He is so interested in all that is going on around him that he may miss out on success by spending too much time on unnecessary projects, or other people and their problems. This subject gets bored quickly and has to make an effort to concentrate on each task and finish what he starts. Being rather wary of committing himself, he leaves the door open so that he can make a quick get-away from a situation which threatens to become too 'heavy'. Astrologers might like to equate loops with the mutable signs, especially Gemini.

TENTED ARCH (Fig. 3.15)

Figure 3.15
The tented arch
finger print

The energy flows straight up the finger, glancing neither to the left nor the right. A subject with a few of these would be straightforward, straight talking and straight faced. He could be idealistic, creative or sporting, obsessive about personal projects. The lack of adaptability

makes it hard for him to cope with changing times, and unexpected events might cause him to become temporarily unhinged, especially if there are suppression lines. This subject is highly strung, overenthusiastic, sensitive to criticism but could be very successful for all that. Astrologers might equate this type with the fixed signs of Leo, Scorpio and Aquarius. A tented arch on Jupiter alone adds tenacity to the personality.

PEACOCK'S EYE (Fig. 3.16)

Figure 3.16
The peacock's eye
finger print

This formation rarely appears on more than one or two fingers and not necessarily on both hands. It indicates talent as it combines the intensity of the whorl with the flexibility of the loop. The finger where it appears will show where the talent lies; for instance, if on Mercury, then communication ability (writing and speaking) will be present. It is also supposed to have magical life-saving qualities.

Lines which run across the fingers overlaying the print pattern come with age; in a young person they indicate fatigue or weakness.

SOME PROBLEM PRINTS

Fig. 3.17

(a) Arch with suppression ridges which

show a defeatist mentality, a person who holds himself back from a challenge, not good at coping with problems.

(b) A 'string of pearls' formation indicating frustration, resentment.

Fig. 3.18
A whorl (see page 43) which is just about visible. This print was taken from an elderly lady whose sight is failing and is similar to the palmar pattern of the insomniac.

Fig. 3.19
(a) The suppression lines are displaced to one side showing the 'push-pull' effect on the character, making him want to be assertive and tough, but more likely to be bombastic.

(b) This is a displaced arch pattern. The core is a whorl which shows a 'know it all' attitude to life, but the slightly off-centre placement indicates angry outbursts rather than quiet self-confidence.

(c) The lines pressing down on the whorl add an almost arched look to the formation implying a lack of self-confidence under the blustering outer manner — in short a prize bully!

Fig. 3.20
Top phalange. Warts signify long-term stress, in this case mental anguish (see Chapter 11).

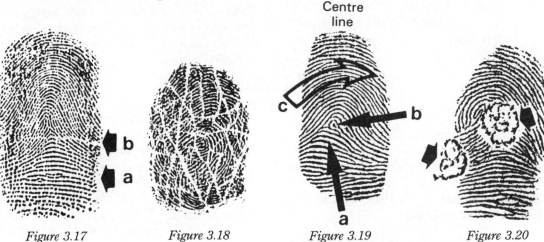

Figure 3.17   Figure 3.18   Figure 3.19   Figure 3.20

Brief Breakdown of the Phalanges

TOP, MIDDLE, LOWER
1st   Mental, spiritual, emotional.
2nd   Application of ideas, practicalities, putting things into action.
3rd   Physically doing things, material matters.

LONG PHALANGES

JUPITER
1st   Emotional, sensitive, religious.
2nd   Practical worker, determined, ambitious.
3rd   Worldly, inflexible, self-indulgent, a flashy dresser, has an urge to rule.

SATURN
1st   Loner, withdrawn personality, prudent, suicidal.
2nd   Lone worker, cautious, money minded, interested in agricultural pursuits.
3rd   Hoards, mistrusts, greedy.

APOLLO
1st Mental stress in creative people.

2nd Likes beauty, musical, good designer, idealist.

3rd Likes luxury, trendy artist, makes money from showbusiness-type work, materially successful.

MERCURY

1st Nervy, abstract thinker with unusual mind, studious, literary.

2nd Worker in business, rational.

3rd Restless, fraudulent trickster, skilled but cunning.

SHORT PHALANGES

JUPITER

1st Materialistic, shallow, untrusting.

2nd Lacks ambition, lazy.

3rd Low self-image, hides away from life, wants to be left alone with own interests.

SATURN

1st Resignation, contentment, calm, steady personality.

2nd Insignificant, ignorant, time-waster.

3rd Economical, frugal, mean.

APOLLO

1st Lacks artistic feelings and ideas.

2nd No inspiration or potential, may be a failure.

3rd Lack of skills in art, crafts and mechanics.

MERCURY

1st Lack of alertness, mentally lazy, dull.

2nd Lack of initiative.

3rd Simplicity, gullibility (Malcolm says that's him!)

Crease lines across the fingertips show exhaustion and misery. Crease lines up the 2nd and 3rd phalanges show a temporary state of fatigue.

Nails and Temperament

The finger nails are an excellent indicator of a person's current state of health but there is also some information about personality which can be gleaned from them. The following descriptions presuppose that the subjects are not suffering from any physical or mental illness.

WIDE SHORT NAILS (Fig. 3.21)

Figure 3.21

High energy level, the energy is quickly reflected back down the finger. These subjects have a quick temper but are equally quick to forgive. Their reactions are fast, their wit is sharp, as are their tongues. Sexually and emotionally aggressive, they are prone to jealousy and possessiveness. They like to argue the point and can be sharply critical. They are not too interested in the feelings of others, especially when in a competitive situation. If *they* are proved wrong, they sulk — they do not take criticism kindly. If the nails are very small the outlook is narrow, bigoted (especially if the head and heart lines are close together).

WIDE LONG NAILS (Fig. 3.22)

Figure 3.22

The energy takes longer to be reflected — this shows caution, sense, reserve. These people can be nervy but have a frank and kindly nature; they are sympathetic, emotional and reliable in affections. They prefer practical jobs and creative pursuits to sports; they are deep thinkers but they lack vigour and competitive spirit.

WIDE ROUNDED NAILS (Fig. 3.23)

Figure 3.23

The nail is as wide as it is long but rounded at the moons; the energy flows smoothly around it. These placid-natured people prefer discussion to argument, may worry but rarely feel tense and angry; they prefer not to be spiteful or hurtful. The flow of energy reflects their gentle and sensible manner. They can become dreamy and detached from reality if they have a long flowing head line.

SHORT FAN-SHAPED NAILS, SPATULATE (Fig. 3.24)

Figure 3.24

The energy flows quickly around the nail. There are two distinct types of nature that go with this nail. One is placid and lacking in vitality, may endure some long drawn-out kind of illness, and if he/she becomes angry, this is probably due to underlying illness. The hands would be small and soft.

If the hands are firm, full of hard-packed fat with deeply-embedded white or blueish nails, there can be an explosive temper-

ament. This person is highly ambitious but also wants to be liked and admired by others. Bigoted, moody, extremely unpleasant at times, although charming when wanting something, this type should take up some extremely competitive kind of sport in order to burn off the excess of tension, competitiveness and sheer nastiness. If the nails lie on top of the fingers as if they were not securely attached, the subject will have a whining, complaining manner and will be too lazy to engage in sport. The competitiveness is there nevertheless and the nature is just as nasty.

LONG NARROW NAILS (Fig. 3.25)

Figure 3.25

These are usually only found on women. The energy flows quickly past the nail on either side. A lot of flesh showing on either side of the nail shows selfishness. These people can be superficially charming, even a little babyish at times, but make no mistake, they are ambitious, possessive and materialistic. They like the good things of life without expending too much effort to get them. The narrower the nail, the more touchy they are. If the nails grow long, the more mercenary they are, especially if there are also whorls on Jupiter and Apollo.

CURVED CLAW-LIKE NAILS

These are long and narrow nails, similar to Fig. 3.25, but they curve in a claw-like fashion. They imply greed and possessiveness. If anyone tries to get in these subjects' way, there is every likelihood of their talons being used to clear their path once again.

48THE LIVING HAND

There are some racial indications here. If the subject is black, brown or Jewish, the curved nails are a natural feature which, in this case, doesn't mean greed, selfishness, etc.

VERY SMALL NAILS

These indicate poor resistance to disease but also a weak, self-centred nature. There could be a foul temper, especially if the nails are very pink. This person could also be overcritical of others, sarcastic and hurtful.

KNOTTED FINGERS (Fig. 3.26)

People with knots on their fingers are well organized and capable of meticulous work, even if the fingers are basically short. In normal non-arthritic hands, knots are usually only found on the second knuckle, as illustrated. These are sometimes called knots of material order. If there are knots

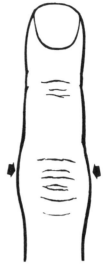

Figure 3.26

on the first knuckles, these are called knots of mental order which belong to a philosophical person.

CHAPTER FOUR

The Thumb

The Overall Picture

If the thumb is large and strong, the subject will be vigorous, extroverted and strong-willed. If it is small and weak, the subject will be ailing, introverted and lacking in both courage and 'oomph'.

The thumb is on the radial side of the hand so it affects the way one deals with life in practical terms. It shows the measure of strength, will power, the desire for challenge or need for a quiet life, plus the ability to cope; it therefore modifies the whole hand.

A newly-born baby holds its thumb close to the fingers. At about two to three months, the baby begins to reach out and touch objects around it; by then it is stronger, more accustomed to its surroundings and beginning to look outwards at the world around it. When it feels miserable it may suck its thumb for comfort — people of any age can regress to this habit.

A thumb which is tucked into the hand is a sure sign of insecurity, depression, severe lack of confidence and helplessness, especially if the fingers are held tightly together and curled around the thumb. When someone is near to death, as the life force ebbs away, the thumb will drop into the hand. A thumb which is held naturally is a sure sign of confidence and strength.

The thumb is such a strong indicator of the force (or otherwise) of our character and behaviour that some eastern palmists give a complete reading from it. If we want to see whether our subject has any kind of initiative, driving force and how this is used, it must be examined closely.

LENGTH (Fig. 4.1)

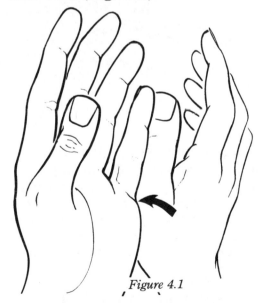

Figure 4.1

A quick method of determining the length is to place the knuckle at the bottom of the thumb in the hollow which lies just below the Mercury finger (the angle of dexterity). The thumb and Mercury finger should be near enough the same length.

LENGTH (Fig. 4.2a)
Alternatively, the thumb, when placed alongside the hand, should reach halfway up the third phalange of the Jupiter finger.

SHORT THUMB (Fig. 4.2b)
On an otherwise strong hand this shows weakness in the character, a tendency toward subordination. People with short thumbs do not have a strong will of their own, they are easily led and do not have much control over their own lives. If the thumb is stubby there is a lack of sensitivity; these people are aggressive, ruthless and cruel; they seek power and abuse it.

LONG THUMB (Fig. 4.2c)
This denotes a rational approach to life. These people are born leaders and have natural staying power. The more refined the shape of the thumb, the more refined the person.

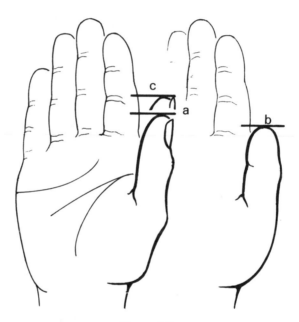

Figure 4.2

HIGH-SET THUMB WITH AN ACUTE ANGLE (Fig. 4.3a)
An angle of 45° or less indicates a nature which is overcontrolled, a tight rein on the emotions, a restrictive, unadventurous and habit-bound attitude to life with pre-judgement of situations and small-mindedness.

LOW-SET THUMB WITH AN OBTUSE ANGLE (Fig. 4.3b)
An angle of 90° indicates an extrovert, adventurous and easily-inspired nature, a love of new ventures. The subject is easy going, optimistic, charming and independent. An angle of about 80° brings a sense of responsibility and qualities of leadership; over 80° indicates irresponsibility, foolhardiness.

NON-ALIGNMENT OF THUMB (Fig. 4.4a)
Thumb facing the fingers like a sergeant facing his troops — the subject keeps

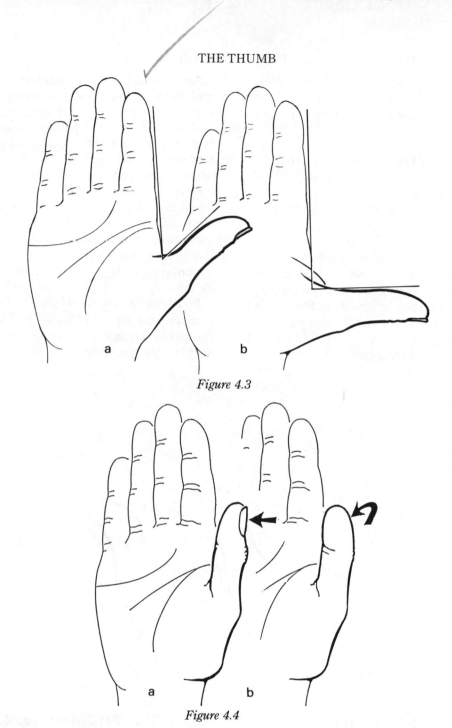

Figure 4.3

Figure 4.4

himself in line. He may play the fool but he knows what he is doing.

ALIGNMENT OF THUMB (Fig. 4.4b)

Thumb nail showing on the back of the hand when the hand is at rest indicates

enthusiasm, spontaneity and enjoyment of life.

STIFF THUMB (Fig. 4.5a)

If the thumb is straight at the back, there is a strong sense of self-discipline suggesting a consistent and persistent worker with an inflexible and rigid outlook. If the top phalange bends inwards toward the fingers, narrow-mindedness, selfishness and stinginess.

SUPPLE THUMB (Fig. 4.5b)

Known as the 'spendthrift thumb'. These people go into a shop to buy an item and end up buying something totally different. An impulsive and generous nature, if the top phalange as it appears in side view is flat (Fig. 4.9d). These people are entertainers with dramatic talent, craftsmen, if they have a spatulate top phalange (Fig. 4.8c), and if they have a weak thumb they can be a sucker for a hard luck story. These people have active minds but like an easy life and can be physically lazy.

Subjects with a large thumb and a heavy top phalange will be determined, hardworking, responsible and civilized. They have the peculiarity of being very generous to themselves but not always willing to see that others also have needs. They enjoy making large and important purchases both for themselves and their family but are bored by the need to give up money for mundane necessities. This is extremely frustrating for those who have to live with them. They love to be in the centre of the action and to have full attention paid to them.

People with supple thumbs have nice manners and are often found working with the public or in sales. People with thick, stiff thumbs are blunt but honest.

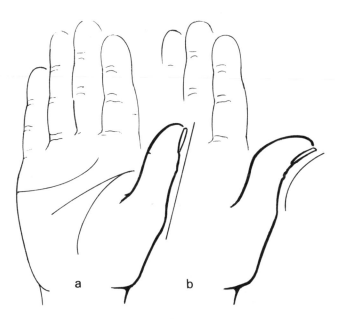

Figure 4.5

TUBULAR THUMB (Fig. 4.6a)

Practical by nature, these people like to buy and use things that fit and work properly.

WAVY THUMB (Fig. 4.6b)

A pleasant exterior but quite a firm nature — these people will not be put upon too much.

CLUBBED THUMB (Fig. 4.6c)

These subjects have no ability to debate or dispute; they either back away from an argument or lose control.

THE ANGLE OF DEXTERITY (Fig. 4.7)

This is also called the angle of rhythm or

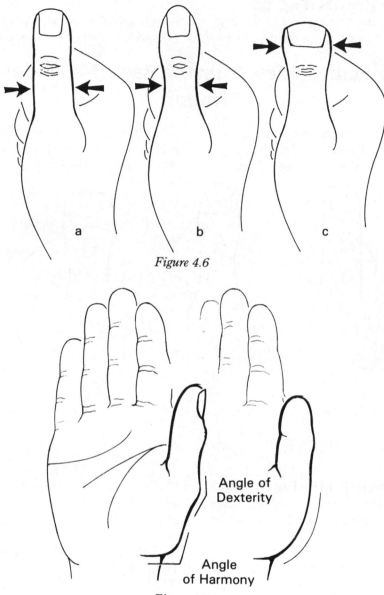

Figure 4.6

Figure 4.7

proficiency. If well developed, the subject is a good craftsman, he will see a job through to its end and will prefer tasks which have a physical rhythm. This may take the form of sports such as tennis or cricket, a love of music or the swinging action that a carpenter uses for sawing or planing.

THE ANGLE OF HARMONY (Fig. 4.7)

These people have a natural sense of the rightness of things and would like beautifully-made furniture, antiques, music or attractive clothes. The greater the length between the two angles, the warmer the personality.

ROUNDED EDGES (Fig. 4.7)

These people are easy going and warm hearted. The energy flows quickly to the thumb giving a quick temper — also they are quick to 'warm up' sexually.

First Phalange: View from the Back (Nail Side) of the Thumb

The nail section of the thumb is concerned with will power. The shape of the phalange shows how determination is used. If this is long, there is great determination which is held under control, also staying power. If short, lack of will-power and self-control.

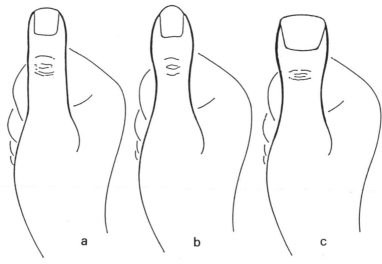

Figure 4.8

SQUARED-OFF TIP (Fig. 4.8a)

Practical, reliable and sensible, these people can be taskmasters but like to lead the way by setting a good example.

CONIC TIP (Fig. 4.8b)

A graceful approach to life: these people are quick to spot weakness in others yet spring to their defence. Easily swayed from a goal, they are impressionable, idealistic.

If very wide at the joint (like Fig. 4.2) but with a point, they will be argumentative, obstinate.

A-SHAPED, SPATULATE TIP (Fig. 4.8c)

The craftsman's thumb indicating a good manual dexterity. If not too thick, there will be sensitivity, creativity but all put to a practical use (squared-off tip).

Side View of Top Phalange

WEDGE SHAPED (Fig. 4.9a)

There is a pronounced knuckle at the back end of the wedge. These subjects are bloody minded, they won't give an inch, and therefore make good barristers, but could be fanatics, religious maniacs etc.

BULBOUS SHAPE (Fig. 4.9b)

With these subjects their basic appetites are near the surface — passionate, obstin-

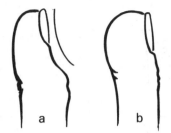

a   b   c   d   e

Figure 4.9

ate, lacking in refinement. With a high mount of Venus, they will be ruthless in pursuits.

ROUNDED (Fig. 4.9c)

The most commonly-found shape — nice balance between will and authority plus the ability to relate to the will of other people.

FLAT SHAPE (Fig. 4.9d)

Refined, gentle but lacking in energy. If the tip is conic, the subject will get his or her own way without other people really noticing what is going on, either by hinting or chiselling away until the other person gives in. An old palmistry book of ours says of this flat shape, 'the possessor will yield to affection' — which probably means that they do not hold back for long before jumping into bed with the nearest and most persistent suitor.

SPOKE-SHAVED SHAPE (Fig. 4.9e)

This shape indicates a need to be loved and appreciated. Refined, pleasant but could be too willing to give way for the sake of approval.

Second Phalange

THICK, STRAIGHT (Fig. 4.10a)

The energy flows unimpeded up and down the thumb. This subject is straight to the point and does not like fuss. A policeman or judge would need this kind of thumb as they deal with the facts, the actual evidence. This subject reasons things out by what he can read or see, things must be black or white, visible, practical and tangible. He would follow conventional religious views. There is a tendency to bluntness, even tactlessness or rudeness because these people do not see beneath the surface, but they are themselves truthful and therefore trustworthy.

LENGTH OF THE FIRST AND SECOND PHALANGES

The two phalanges should be approximately the same length. If the second phalange is longer than the first it reveals one who is more of a thinker than a doer. He may spend so much time rationalizing that he never actually gets down to the task in hand. If the top phalange is markedly longer, the subject will act before thinking.

WAISTED PHALANGE (Fig. 4.10b)

The energies are knocked from one side to the other before reaching the will power. These subjects are analytical, subtle thinkers who can look beneath the surface of life. They hate to swallow anything whole, but need to question and ponder over things — less practical, more spiritual.

It is interesting to watch these two types in discussion. The thick phalange will quote, 'I read this or saw that' whilst the waisted phalange would say, 'In my experience, I found . . .'

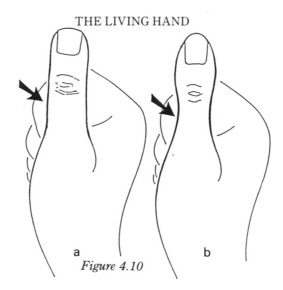

a   b

Figure 4.10

PRINT PATTERNS ON THE THUMB

See Chapter 3 on finger prints for a more detailed explanation, this is just a quick guide.

Whorl   Selfish, original, ambitious.
Loop   Team-worker, adaptable, pleasant, conventional.

Arch   Withdrawn, shy, restricted personality.
Double loop Tries to please everyone at once, likes people but needs own company. This often shows up on the hands of psychic people for some reason.

The Base of the Thumb

This is the powerhouse of the thumb, where its energies are stored. It is part of the mount of Venus (see Chapter 2) and represents feelings and desires before they are put into action. Venus embraces the physical world, the life force: therefore, the thicker that mount the more forceful the personality; the thinner the mount, the more diplomatic and ready to give way to others. This shows whether the subject is logical or instinctive, tactful or thoughtless.

The area all around the base of the thumb, leading down towards the heel of the hand both on the back and the front, can be used to assess stamina, resistance to disease and the strength of the subject both in terms of health and of temperament. The mount of Venus is the storehouse of the body's reserves of energy; it is encircled by the life line which is itself associated with the physical and mental health of the subject. The 'mouse' is the area which can be seen and felt at the *back* of the thumb when the hand is closed.

STRONG (Fig. 4.11)

A large, firm mouse would suggest a subject whose current state of health is good and who has a naturally good resistance to disease plus good powers of recovery from illness. By nature he is restless, assertive, possibly even aggressive — only really happy working in a demanding job. If the head line is firm and straight with a well-developed Jupiter finger, there will be good executive abilities. If the knuckle of dexterity is well shaped and the percussion also well developed this subject would make a successful competitive sportsman.

Figure 4.11

If the mount of Venus is high and firm when the hand is relaxed, there will be a good flow of blood through the circulatory system. The finger nails should have well developed moons for a strong constitution. These people are robust and passionate; they enjoy sports and other outdoor activities which give them the opportunity to sop up some of their ample energy and release some of their natural aggression in competition with others. They can be selfish, putting their own interests first, being in too much of a hurry to get on with life to stop in mid-stream and deal with the wants of others.

WEAK (Fig. 4.12)

A floppy mouse points to a *currently* poor state of health, possibly someone who is recovering from illness or an operation or who has a generally weak constitution. A flattish mount of Venus belongs to someone who likes to keep the mind occupied rather than take part in physical exercise. If the mount of Venus if exceptionally thin and soft, the subject would either be lethargic or have a particularly inward-looking nervous type of temperament. These

people are sometimes cold and indifferent, unable to give or receive love, especially if the heart line is weak looking, short, or does not curve upwards at all.

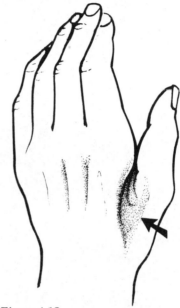

Figure 4.12

If when the hand is relaxed there is a definite hollow where a muscle should be (see Fig. 4.13) this would imply muscle

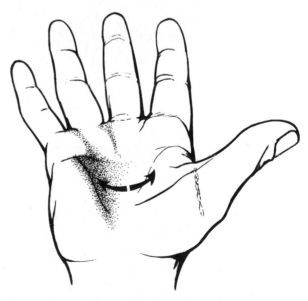

Figure 4.13

atrophy which could be the indicator of oncoming disease. Look at the major lines for signs of any neurological changes; if there are none, then look for diabetes.

CHAPTER FIVE

The Language of Gesture

How the fingers are held and used

It is always interesting to see how people use their hands, also how their hands are placed when relaxed. A palmist can learn a great deal by creating a calm atmosphere during the reading and then glancing from time to time at the client's hands; it may even be possible to work out why someone has come to visit whilst chatting and putting the client at ease.

You may find it difficult to place your *own* fingers in some of the poses which we have shown but it you acquire the habit of watching other people's hands, you will see that hands *do* fall naturally into these shapes. Take notice of people who are under stress and also people who are relaxed. Watch your friends on social occasions when they are happy, when angry or irritable. There is no research like your own research — talk to people whose hands seem to fall into odd poses, and see what mood they are in and what is on their mind.

A palmist must compare *both* of the subject's hands closely. The dominant hand will show the *current* situation, worries and problems; the minor hand will show the *underlying* influences, problems and the subject's habitual manner of thinking. When a client first comes in to the room, he may hold his hands in one way; later,

when confident, he could hold them quite differently.

FINGERS HELD STRAIGHT OR CURLED INTO A FIST-LIKE SHAPE (Fig. 5.1)

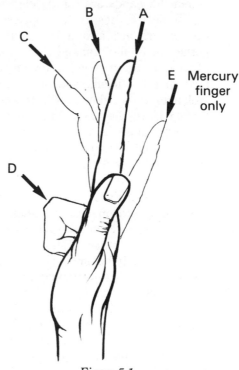

Figure 5.1

A   Fingers which are held straight out show that the subject is self-assured, easy to get along with and optimistic. He may be a touch reckless. People whose fingers are splayed open are receptive to new ideas, they do not pre-judge.

B   If the top phalanges are curled over a little the subject is self-assured, but common sense gives him a slightly more cautious attitude when in unfamiliar situations. If all the fingers are held tightly together in a sort of 'karate-chop', with no light showing between them, the subject is holding back until he has assessed the situation. When he relaxes, he will loosen the fingers and let light through them.

C   If the first and second phalanges are curved, the subject feels that he is not walking on safe ground, he is not sure of his facts. If the fingers are also held tightly together, he is self-absorbed, slightly introverted.

D   When the hands are tightly clenched, the subject is desperate, hopeless. If the fingers are also held tightly together, he or she is unable to cope with life and afraid of showing any emotion for fear of criticism, rejection or even violence. If in addition the thumb is tucked in to the hand, the subject is probably close to a nervous breakdown. People who work with severely maltreated and unhappy children are familiar with the sight of a tucked-in thumb. It is a sign of self-protection in the face of extreme circumstances.

E   If the Mercury finger falls behind, away from the others, in the fashion of a Victorian lady holding a tea-cup, then the subject is self-contained and stubborn. There is very little desire to give and take, there is only one standpoint: his own. If there is a strong thumb, then the subject feels that he is always right; his mind has been long since made up.

SPACING BETWEEN FINGERS

The spaces between the fingers are usually uneven; some fingers cling together, some wander off on their own. Take a look at both hands and compare the spacing while they are relaxed.

SPACE BETWEEN JUPITER AND SATURN FINGERS (Fig. 5.2)

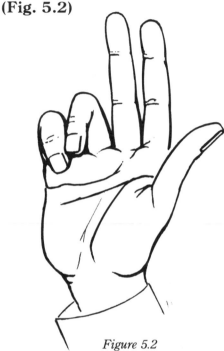

Figure 5.2

This is the active and outgoing radial side of the hand which shows the ability to think for oneself. This subject may listen to advice but in the last resort he always needs to make his own decisions.

If the Mercury and Apollo fingers curl over into a slight fist shape, the emotional side of life will be difficult. This person may have a disappointing home life, or may find personal relations difficult. However, when at work he performs well and feels in control of the situation. This kind of hand may belong to the hardworking owner of a small business who loves the day-to-day challenge of work but either tunes out when at home or is rarely at ease in personal or emotional situations.

THE LANGUAGE OF GESTURE

SATURN AND APOLLO FINGERS HELD CLOSELY TOGETHER (Fig. 5.3)

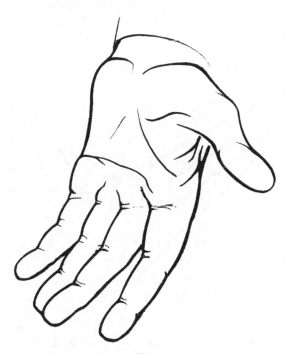

Figure 5.3

This type of posture is very commonly seen nowadays — it shows the need for security and understanding. If the subject has a strong thumb, he will be able to stand up for himself and be able to cope. There could be conflict between the demands of family and career, or there could be a desire to work primarily for job satisfaction rather than just for money.

SPACE BETWEEN SATURN AND APOLLO

This person may be a loner, the type who lives in the past and hates planning for the future. The characteristic v shape where the top two phalanges are apart shows signs of rebelliousness. This person probably did not 'fit in' while at school. If there are whorl patterns on the finger tips then this person is definitely *not* a team worker.

SPACE BETWEEN APOLLO AND MERCURY FINGERS (Fig. 5.4)

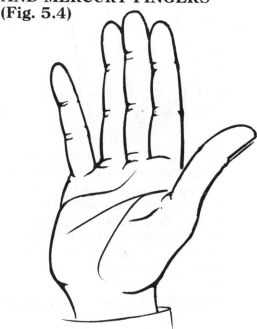

Figure 5.4

This indicates the ability to act independently. Watch these people while they are speaking; they will be putting their own interpretation on the conversation. The conductor of an orchestra who holds his Mercury finger away from the others will interpret the music to reflect his own ideas. These people also need to get away from other people from time to time to recharge their mental batteries. There could be a sense of loneliness here.

Sample Analyses

FINGER TIPS RESTING LIGHTLY ON A TABLE (Fig. 5.5)

This is the same basic shape as Fig. 5.3. Notice that the Jupiter and Saturn fingers

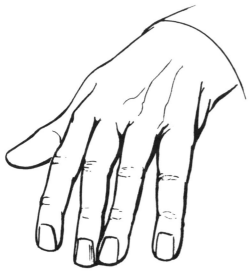

Figure 5.5

are more arched; the arched Jupiter is showing an inner lack of confidence and the Saturn some inadequacy when coping with everyday problems plus a need for security and understanding. It is by looking at these details that the palmist begins to build up a mental picture of his subject's abilities, weak spots and the depth of his feelings.

A WOMAN'S HAND 1 (Fig. 5.6)

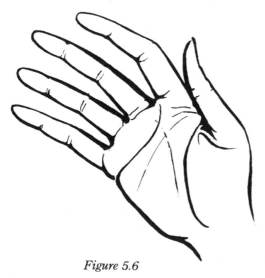

Figure 5.6

The fingers here are evenly spaced but curved. The open fingers show an open

mind. The Jupiter finger is more curved than the others which shows some uncertainty in her direction. The subject wants to be told the truth about herself and her life and she will not hide anything from the palmist. The thumb which is lying close to the hand shows a desire to co-operate rather than to push herself forward.

A WOMAN'S HAND 2 (Fig. 5.7)

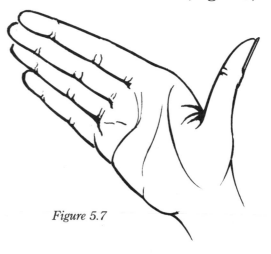

Figure 5.7

Similar to Fig. 5.6 but this time the fingers are held close together and straight. The thumb is sticking out.

People like this can be seen on television discussion programmes; they are confident, their closed fingers show that they do not want to be questioned or contradicted, their minds are closed to fend off criticism and hide any sign of inadequacy. They do not wish to show emotion, they think it a sign of weakness. If the thumb is held away from the hand, they are 'in charge'. If the first phalange of the thumb turns back they may *appear* to be assertive and extrovert but this may be covering shyness, selfish motives, greed etc.

A WOMAN'S HAND 3 (Fig. 5.8)

This illustration shows limp hands turned inwards toward each other. This posture is a nervous defensive reaction which shows that the emotional energy level is low. It

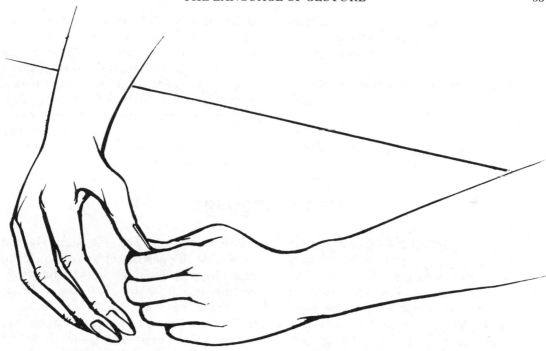

Figure 5.8

would be a good idea to look at the life line in the minor hand for corroboration of this. Note the left hand is massaging the thumb of the right; this is a form of reflexology. You see people massaging their finger tips while thinking what to say.

HANDS ON THE TABLE (Fig. 5.9)

A man sits before you and places his hands on the table. The spaces between the fingers in both hands are equal, indicating a balanced open mind. It is rare that one

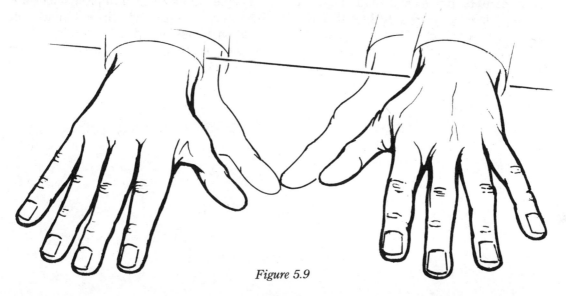

Figure 5.9

actually finds fingers equally spaced like these. If he chooses to lay his hands flat on the table this shows that the inner and outer self are balanced and the mind is relaxed. If the palms are raised a little this means he is conscious of his surroundings and environment.

Arched hands show uncertainty. If the hands are placed wide apart, this is a sign of an active nature — a person who likes to get things moving. The closer the hands are placed, the more thought he will give before acting. If the two thumbs are extended and touching each other, and both hands are aligned symetrically, this person is unconsciously aware of everything that is happening in his environment, every movement in the room. He could overreact to a situation and sometimes pick up on irrelevant details.

Hand Language

People who are trying to be convincing, or to sell something, use their hands in a 'giving' motion whilst at the same time nodding their heads. Charles Dickens's hateful character, Uriah Heep, is depicted 'washing his hands' and really manipulative people can actually be seen doing this! Sometimes 'hand washing' is a sign of severe distress. It is certainly a sign of desperation when the thumbs are tucked tightly in and the arms held stiffly down at the sides. This behaviour is most noticeable among children who are terrified and miserable. If adults display this kind of behaviour, one can be sure that they are either under the ultimate kind of stress or being abused by mental and physical cruelty. There may be a feeling that the subject has a history of being a battered child. A rocking motion is another indication of utter despair.

From pre-history onwards, human beings have used the gesture of an open palm to prove friendly intentions; it is an automatic gesture which shows that they are not carrying a weapon. Those who want to be understood 'plead' with their hands, but this device is also used by the manipulative person who is determined to have his way and at the same time look as if he is being terribly reasonable, even philanthropic! A 'roly-poly' or a 'stacking-up' motion with the hands held in front of the subject also means that he is looking for understanding, and if the motions become wilder, he is not getting it — or is being deliberately misunderstood.

People who wag their Jupiter finger are being bossy. Curled fingers may, in addition to all that has been said in this chapter, be temporarily caused by hot or dry skin.

CHAPTER SIX

Energy Rhythms; Timing; An Introduction to the Lines

Energy Rhythms on the Hands

There is a common belief that the body renews itself every seven years. There is no real foundation for this belief; indeed, we know that some parts of the body, such as bone, change very slowly after puberty, whilst the soft tissue restores itself rapidly — especially the liver. Nevertheless, there does seem to be some basis for this, even if it is only a kind of imaginary psychological timing mechanism.

This arbitrary rhythm shows up in a sudden increase in the number of lines which arrive on the hand adjacent to the fate line or the Apollo line at particular points along their paths. The body seems to build up an excess of nervous, emotional and physical energies which have to be released somewhere. These energies can galvanize people into action and cause them to change their lives in a positive way, e.g. change their job or house or start their own business. A marriage which has never been all that good can suddenly feel stifling at these tension-filled times, causing the subject to make that long dreamed of break or to take up with someone else. It is also amazing how these times can acutally coincide with external events such as redundancy, promotion, the birth of a child or the spouse walking out. If the energy is

suppressed for too long, pressure builds up which will cause unusual behaviour or be internalized into mental or physical ailments. This energy will find any seat of weakness in the body and exploit it, just as the wind and tides will work away at cracks

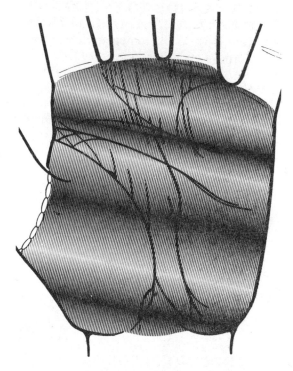

Figure 6.1 Energy rhythms

in a sea wall, ultimately bringing down the whole structure.

One must look at the life line and head line to find out which way this will affect the subject. If there are many lines at the top of the hand, there will be a surge in old age which will be too much for the body to take; this would probably cause the subject to die quite suddenly.

Fig. 6.1 gives a suggestion of the kind of wave pattern which can be seen on a hand. We suggest that you take a look at a few hand prints and then draw horizontal bands across them to show the sections which are most 'busy'. The more of these 'companion' lines there are, the more tension the subject has to cope with. An indication of a positive use of this energy is in the effort lines which rise upwards from the life line; these lines can give some valuable clues to the timing of the rhythm in each individual person's hand.

SIMPLE GUIDE TO ENERGY ON THE FATE AND APOLLO LINES

A   One long, thick companion line gives purpose and aims in life.

B   Two or more short, strong companion lines give change, ambition, restlessness, desires.

C   Many fine lines around Apollo show that the subject is searching for the way forward, is apprehensive and using more energy than the body is producing (look for dots to substantiate this). The searching and apprehension could involve a questioning of the subject's whole way of life; however, it is the *emotional*, relating, family side of life which is probably the uppermost problem.

D   Many fine lines around the fate line may indicate freelance work or stretched physical and financial resources. The subject could be taking on too many obligations; these could be chores for family and friends or financial obligations (see Chapter 10).

E   Many fine lines at the top of the palm are a sign of activity creating energy. These people like to keep busy later in life thereby remaining fit and spry well into old age. Malcolm's old Victorian palmistry book says that if the lines go up into the fingers, the person becomes cantankerous in old age.

This theory of the *rhythm of energies* which appear on the hands fits in with the theories of *transits* which are known to astrologers. The major planets make many cycles, including the well known seven-year cycles, but the times of major stress, achievement and change are as follows:

Saturn sextile age 21.

Neptune sextile age 26.

Saturn return age 29½.

Uranus half-return age 39 — 42

Neptune trine age about 52 — 54.

Saturn return age about 55 — 59.

Uranus return age about 80 — 85.

(Astrology buffs please note that the age ranges given here are approximate in order to allow for the variation in planetary movement and the 'orb' of influence which makes a transit effective before and after it hits the exact conjunction.) There are many other such transits, but these are the most regular and the most obvious ones which affect every one of us.

Timing on the Hand

INSTRUCTIONS FOR CALCULATION

Many palmistry books try to show the passage of time on the hands by dividing the lines up into equal segments, but the hand is *not* a mechanical instrument so timing cannot be calibrated in this manner. **Joys and sorrows which are particularly intense** *appear* **to take a longer period of time to occur on the hand than they do in real life.** The *impact* of an experience upon the mind and body leaves its mark just as the memory of the trauma lingers; it remains in the hand when subsequent, less emotive events have long been forgotten. As we grow older the years appear to fly by; this is reflected in the crowded spacing of the years at the northern end of the palm.

LIFE LINE AND FATE LINE

This is complex because both lines are influenced by each other at the southern end of the hand. The timing goes *up and down* the life line for health and energy, and *up* the hand when influenced by the events which show up on the fate line.

LIFE LINE AND HEAD LINE

The section of the head line which is under the Jupiter and Saturn fingers shows the competition between the requirements of the mind and the body while the subject is in the process of growing up.

QUICK METHOD OF TIMING ON THE HAND

Look at the hand with the fingers together and the thumb relaxed and away from the hand.

(a) Fig. 6.2
A line dropped down from the middle of the Jupiter finger meets the *life line* at approximately 15 – 17 years of age.

(b) Fig. 6.3
A line dropped down between the Jupiter and Saturn fingers meets the *life line* at approximately 22 – 25 years of age.

(c) Fig. 6.4
A line dropped down the middle of the Saturn finger meets the *life line* at approximately 30 – 35 years.

(d) Fig. 6.5
Draw an imaginary line across the hand from the angle of dexterity (arrowed) and at right angles to the line dropping down from Saturn. This represents approximately 45 years of age on the *life line* but only 23 – 25 years on the *fate line*.

(e) Fig. 6.6
Take two more equal spaces down the *life line* to reach the age of 55 – 60 years; this

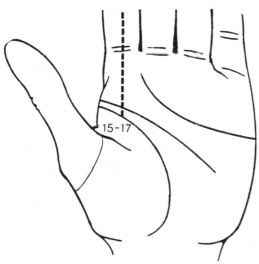

Figure 6.2

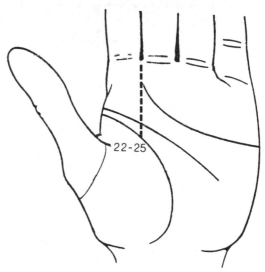

Figure 6.3

corresponds to 20–23 years on the *fate and life lines*. The next equal spacing down the

life line will take you to the age of 18–19 years on the *fate line* only.

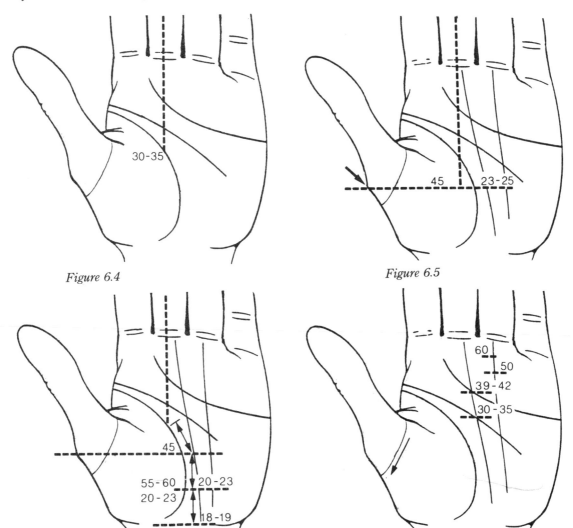

Figure 6.4

Figure 6.5

Figure 6.6

Figure 6.7

LIFE LINE AND FATE LINE
There is a definite relationship between the *life line* and the *fate line* at around the age of 20; therefore an island at that point can suggest a low depressive period at the age of 20 and an illness at around 60.

TIMING ON THE FATE LINE (Fig. 6.7)
The age of 30–35 years is reached on the

fate line at the point where it meets the *head line*. The age of 39–42 years is reached on the *fate line* where it meets the *heart line*. Half way between the heart line and the crease line at the bottom of the Apollo finger is 50 years of age; three-quarters of the way between the heart line and the crease at the bottom of the Apollo finger is 60 years of age.

Figure 6.8

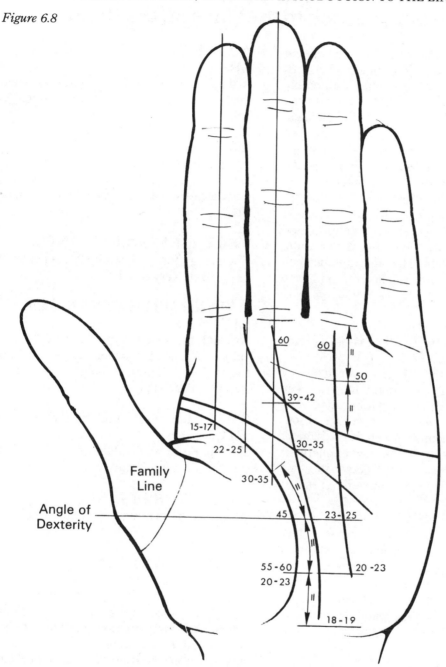

FATE LINE AND APOLLO LINE
The timing between the *fate line* and the *Apollo line* is more or less straight across the hand. They run parallel to each other but follow the contours of the head and heart lines.

TIMING ON THE FAMILY LINE (Fig. 6.7)
This follows the arc of the *life line* downwards.

An Introduction to the Lines on the Hand

For centuries palmists have enjoyed talking about lines on the hand, giving them names and characteristics, sometimes with barely a glance at the picture they really portray. Lines are controlled by the nerve endings; they give a physical computer printout of the life and development of each one of us. The lines show our order of priorities and the value which we give to ourselves and our activities. They pick out the environmental influences upon us and our reaction to those around us, also the depth of the feelings which we have toward our mate, family and friends. They display our dedication to a career or job and our ability to handle it.

HOW TO LOOK AT THE LINES ON THE HAND

Try to imagine the lines as a river of energy flowing from the wrist to the fingers. Deep lines can cope with more power; this makes for a positive type of personality. Lines which are unblemished and fairly straight offer no resistance to the flow of energies. This gives purpose to the personality and makes for a relatively trouble-free life.

CONTINUOUS LINES

These show continuity in life. An unbroken fate line belongs to someone who stays for years in the same job. An unbroken Apollo line belongs to someone who remains in the same house or area for years. An unbroken life line tells much the same story. These people do not break new ground.

BENDS IN THE LINES

These show the movement of life's vital forces to be slower and more changeable.

LINES WHICH MERGE TOGETHER OR RUN PARALLEL

This will help the subject.

A LINE SPLITTING INTO A 'Y' SHAPE

A dividing of the ways: this shows where there are decisions to be taken, choices to be made.

ISLANDS

A splitting of energy in two different directions, also difficulties in life depending on where the island is found (see Chapter 11).

VERY FINE MAJOR LINES

The energy flow is restricted: this person is likely to be very touchy.

A HAND WITH CLEAR-CUT LINES

An 'old fashioned' type of hand — this subject has old-fashioned values and likes to conform. There usually is a strong straight health line.

TASSELS, SQUARES, CROSSES ETC.

Please see the individual chapter sections on each of the relevant lines.

TRANSVERSE LINES

Awkward influences put upon people by others, problems, setbacks and decisions.

DOTS ON ANY LINE

These are always important, and their effect can be judged by the places where they are found. Dots are small craters which suck away energy from the line they are situated on. This shows anguish, anxiety or physical stress, illness etc. (see Chapter 12).

MANY FINE LINES GROUPED AROUND A LINE OR REPLACING IT ALTOGETHER AT SOME POINT

These draw energy away from the main

line and could be termed 'searching lines' because they show both the age at which the confusion occurs and the sphere of life which is confused. At this particular point in time, people cannot see the wood for the trees and waste valuable strength thinking of all the possibilities or they may react by overeating, drinking etc. without doing anything positive to sort out their problems. This kind of situation is commonly found on the fate line, but if the subject actually tackles these problems in a positive manner, it is amazing how quickly these tiny lines appear to peel themselves off the hands leaving just two or three stronger and more determined lines.

COLOURED PATCHES OF SKIN WHICH INFLUENCE THE LINES

When a hand has a minimum of lines plus an area of skin with a nicotine-coloured patch, the subject's life is not fully under his control during the period of time shown on the hand. The subject may have had a spell in the services or even in prison. There may be a period of depression or a health problem which is severe enough to be memorable (see Chapter 11). There are other marks which indicate these specific problems, e.g. peculiarly-shaped islands which show the experienced palmist periods of time when the subject felt enclosed and shut off from normal life. This *could* be caused by a spell in prison or in hospital; another example would be a woman who had felt unhappy or enclosed whilst at home with small children. Obviously this situation could feel like 'prison' to one woman but be a time of joy for another — it all depends on the character of the woman, plus the attitude of her husband and family at this time. Another example is of an unhappy spell in a stultifying job.

DO THE LINES ON THE HAND CHANGE?

The answer is *YES*. When a palmist looks at a hand, he sees the picture of the subject's life *at the time of the reading*. Lines do grow, weaken and disappear altogether.

Health problems will cause some lines to dive under the skin or fade away, especially the fate or Apollo lines. Small vertical lines under the skin may become reddish or vein-blueish in colour.

CHAPTER SEVEN

The Major Lines and Zones

The Life Line

BASIC INFORMATION

A long, healthy-looking life line allows the energies to flow easily along its length, giving the lucky subject the prospect of a healthy, happy life with little or nothing to worry about. The line should have deeper colour than the rest of the palm when the hand is stretched. White races should have pink lines, coloured races pinkish-brown or brown.

Look at both hands to see if there are any differences between them. A trauma which is obvious on the minor hand and all but invisible on the dominant one, shows that there has been a difficult experience in the past which the subject has forgotten about, but because it is still marked on the minor hand, one can see that it has gone deeply into his subconscious mind.

Remember, hands change all the time in subtle ways, sometimes quite dramatically. Lines come and go all the time. Your hand is a living organism — a **living hand**.

Remember that the minor hand shows what our inner selves want while the dominant hand shows the adaptations that we make. If, for instance, the life line on the minor hand reaches way out into the palm, while on the dominant hand it tucks round the mount of Venus, there will be a

desire to travel, be adventurous and to seek a different way of life from that of the subject's parents. The dominant hand

Figure 7.1 Lines can come and go

shows a conventional stay-at-home life but more success in relationships.

If the life line divides widely at the lower end with one branch curving round Venus and the other reaching out into the palm (see Fig. 7.2) the subject could desire both a

Figure 7.2

secure home life and a job which allows him to travel and have interesting experiences. He could want both security and freedom; **the chances are that the lucky devil could have it all**.

BEGINNINGS

A life line which begins high up near Jupiter (Fig. 7.3a) or throws small branches upwards at its start, indicates both idealism and ambition. If the line also hugs the mount of Venus fairly closely, the person will be intellectual, idealistic and ambitious rather than instinctive. If the line starts lower down and curves fatly round Venus (Fig. 7.3b) the person will be full of life, both homeloving and sociable, also ambitious, probably sexy and intuitive in an instinctive, self-preserving sort of way. For a life line which is tied to the head line, please refer to the section on the head line (p. 78)

Islands near the start of the life line show troubles in childhood and youth. There is a

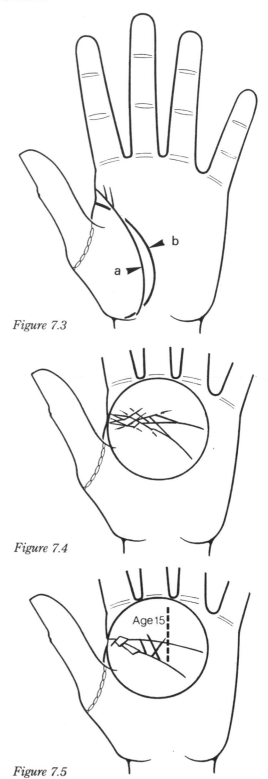

Figure 7.3

Figure 7.4

Figure 7.5

myth that heavy islands at the very beginning of the life line on the radial edge, show some mystery surrounding the subject's birth. In fact, we *can* back up this strange idea as we have come across people who have very angular islands and 'feathering' at this start who have confirmed this (Fig. 7.4). One such person's mother had deliberately registered her at birth as being illegitimate in order to hurt and humiliate the legitimate father!

Straightforward islands are more likely to be caused by illness; a large rather isolated island would indicate a fairly lengthy spell in hospital. A gap between the life and head lines with crisscross lines, islands or short harsh lines barring the way (Fig. 7.5) indicates that the subject was probably looked after by someone other than its parents as a child and was not happy with the arrangement. Unhappiness at school is shown by a 'cat's cradle' effect (see p. 79).

An island or a sudden parting of the ways between the head and life lines with a strong line dropping down from inside the life line (Fig. 7.6) shows a traumatic change of situation during childhood. The dropping line indicates some kind of loss which is consistent with death in the family, parents splitting up, a move of house or a change of school. The implication is that the subject experienced loss of the familiar and had to adjust quickly to an unfamiliar situation.

MIDDLE

This is the section where effort lines frequently appear; their position shows the age at which the subject makes any special effort in life. Events on the life line are often mirrored on the head line (Fig. 7.7), indeed sometimes on the heart line and elsewhere, therefore it is a case of collecting evidence to see what the effort is all about. If there is, for instance, a corresponding upward hook on the head line or a new beginning on the fate line, there could be promotion or a better job. If the effort

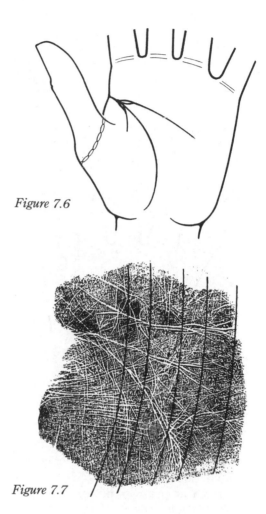

Figure 7.6

Figure 7.7

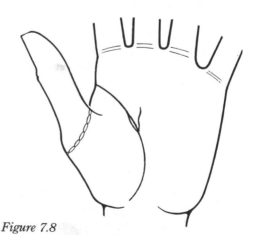

Figure 7.8

line comes at the end of an island or weak patch in the line, it will show that there is a period of illness or emotional suffering from which the person emerges somewhat older and wiser (Fig. 7.8). It proves that personal efforts are made to overcome the problems. It does not matter where these effort lines lead, but the struggle is probably all the harder — and all the more worthwhile — if the lines go toward Saturn.

SHORT LIFE LINE (Fig. 7.9)

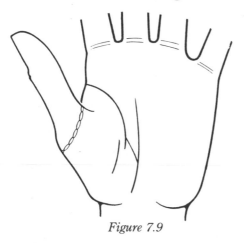

Figure 7.9

Many people, probably about 20 per cent of the population, have broken life lines or lines which appear to be exceptionally short. In practically every case, the fate line becomes a second life line (Fig. 7.9). This picture shows some kind of upsetting change in the subject's life. The most common event these days is divorce. For some reason the life line has a good deal to do with location, where one puts down roots; therefore divorce, with all its uncertainty about how and where one will live, is bound to have a pretty cataclysmic effect on this line.

CASE HISTORY: PAUL AND BRENDA (Fig. 7.10)

Paul and Brenda were a married couple who both had the same formation of a fore-shortened life line which seemed to end at

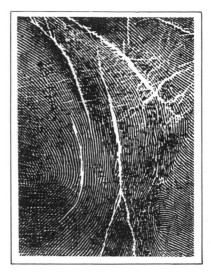

Figure 7.10

the same age point; their fate lines then 'took over' from the life line. It was obvious that both their lives would change drastically because of a traumatic event which would affect both of them at the same time. In the event, a few years later Paul discovered that Brenda was having an affair. It appears that the marriage had not been successful for some time. Paul decided to leave Brenda and their children, thereby causing a sudden unexpected change in both their lives at the same time.

It is worth noting that 'outward' jumps on the life line usually show that the subject is being pushed into concentrating far more intensely on work than he or she had expected to have to do. In the case of Paul, he had to push ahead with his career in order to afford two homes; also he subsequently re-married and started a fresh family. Brenda has not married again, but has developed a successful career for herself, which certainly was not how she had expected her life to proceed. This just goes to show that a short life line is definitely not an indicator of an early death — just the death of a *situation*.

Often a short or broken life line will, in addition to moving over to other parts of the hand, be backed up by extra lines appearing on the mount of Venus. These extra lines strengthen the life line and help the person both to get over the problem and give added physical reserves of strength. There is also a possibility that friends and family are shown to help at that time. The backing line could be a line of Mars, a medial line or just a stray reinforcement line.

LIFE LINE, LOWER-ZONE END WITH LINE OF MARS (Fig. 7.11)

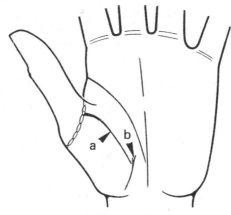

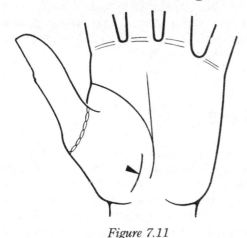

Figure 7.11

This indicates a renewed interest in home and domesticity later in life. A man who has spent his life out at work may retire and find unexpected pleasures in the home and surrounding area. A woman who has struggled with a career and family may be able at last to relax and find pleasure in gardening, cooking or sewing now that she no longer has to do her chores or produce meals while 'on the run'. It means that later in life the priority becomes home, security and emotional understanding once more.

RETURN TO HOME LIFE (Fig. 7.12)

If circumstances have made the subject into a career person as a result of a divorce, then re-marriage could provide a pleasant and comfortable home situation later in life.

Figure 7.12

It is worth looking at the loyalty line (a) to see if this points towards the southern end of the life line, and also at changes on the Apollo line and secondary attachment lines.

If the new line of Mars which backs up the life line at this point has a Y formation on it (b), this is also a sign of re-marriage.

GIVING UP ON LIFE

If the line becomes wispy, tasselled or breaks up into fragments, the subject will either give up on life, preferring to sit back and do nothing, or he may have weak health later in life. This *might* indicate early death, but one must check the lines at the top of the hand to see if life continues. If the life line fades away and then renews itself, there will be a period of weakness followed by a return to health and strength.

SPLITS (Fig. 7.13)

Splits on the southern end of the life line mean some sort of divided loyalty. This can range from the wide split (a), showing a strong home life plus travel and a career, to the narrow split (b) of a mother struggling to work and cope with a young family.

A line which curves round Venus would imply that the subject remains close to the place where he was born and also close to his parents. If there is a split, there will still be contact with the parental family and although the ideas and philosophy of the

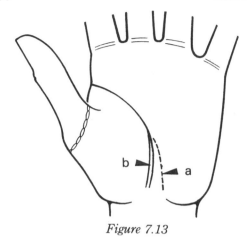

Figure 7.13

two generations could be very different, there would be humorous tolerance between them. If the line sweeps out into the hand, the subject will most probably move far away from his place of birth and/or could have widely divergent attitudes to those of his family. They may never be able to see eye to eye — if they see each other at all!

Reading *up* the line there could be an early illness which has later repercussions, such as rheumatic fever. There may, on the other hand, be a niggling complaint later in life. Splits indicate a split in energies and can refer to health, location or a desire to be in two places at once. It would be a good idea to look to see if there are two family rings, two strong Apollo lines or any other signs of double interests before pronouncing!

The Head Line

BASIC INFORMATION

The head line shows how we use our mind. It can point out damage to the head, throat, neck, shoulders and upper respiratory region plus, of course, mental disturbances. It shows one's habitual manner of thinking and gives information about schooling, studies and the shape of one's career.

A GAP BETWEEN THE HEAD LINE AND THE LIFE LINE (Fig. 7.14)

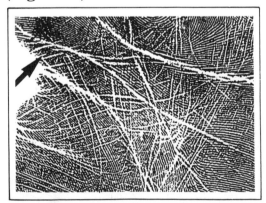

Figure 7.14

If there is a gap at the start of the head line and life line the subject is more likely to be able to take chances in life. He is not too tied to tradition, the ways of his parents or the home. He may leave home early or just be allowed to be himself and develop his personality in a free and easy way. The other meaning is that the person had little to do with his parents during childhood and was forced to become an independent thinker earlier than he wanted to.

BEGINNING (Fig. 7.15)

A 'tied' head line (a) is a head and life line which are joined for about a half an inch (12 mm) or more at their starting point. This belongs to a cautious person who is slow to cut the apron strings whilst a gap between the head and life lines (b) shows a more adventurous type who either leaves home young or has a free and easy relationship with the parents. For confirmation of family pressure look to see if the life and fate lines are also joined at the southern end (c) and if there are family aggravation lines radiating outwards from the mount of

Venus (d). An exceptionally timid person might have a head line which starts *inside* the life line on the mount of Mars (e).

EARLY STRUGGLES (Fig. 7.16 and 7.17)

Islands, bars and jagged, triangular markings at this point show illness or unhappiness in childhood. Small lines which try to bind the parting head and life lines together creating a 'cat's cradle' effect (a) show unhappiness whilst at school or college. (Fig. 7.17) The subject may have hated school, or loved school and seen it as *a place to go to in order to escape from unhappiness at home.* It is possible to spot how old the person was during this time of unhappiness by the position of this effect. If a middle-aged man has a large, triangular or diamond-shaped island just where the head and life line part (b) try asking him if he did national service; he may have enjoyed it, especially if the nearby mount of lower Mars is full (c).

A triangle or diamond-shaped island indicates a period of confinement which may indicate hospital, a bad job, difficult home life or even a period in some sort of institution. The reason for the island is the *feeling* of imprisonment which it gives.

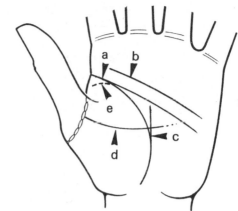

Figure 7.15

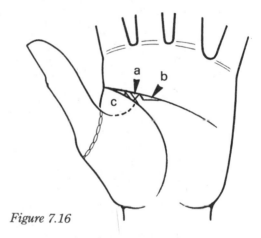

Figure 7.16

Figure 7.17

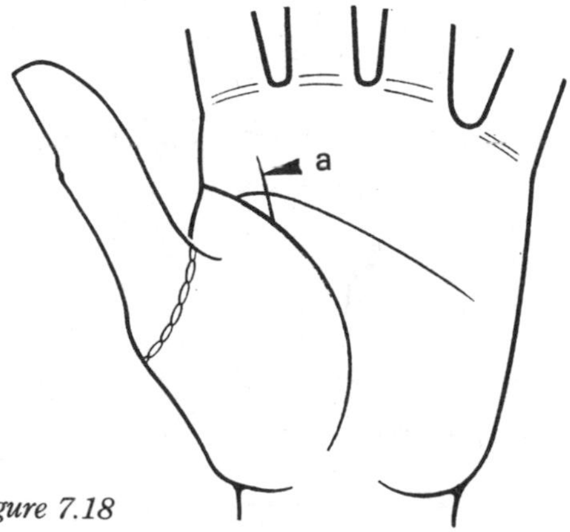

ISLANDS AND EFFORT LINES (Fig. 7.18)

A classic give-away for unhappiness or lack

Figure 7.18

of satisfaction at secondary school is the appearance of effort lines on the life line (a) as soon as it becomes free of the head line. If the head line rises or throws up effort lines here, the person is delighted to leave his adolescence and his schooldays behind him. He begins to blossom intellectually and to take the first meaningful strides in his career.

MIDDLE (Fig. 7.19)

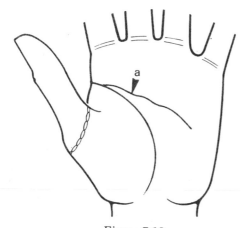

Figure 7.19

This is the practical section of the head line. A strong clear line shows a good mind and healthy upper-body area. A wavy line (a) shows that the subject has difficulty in sustaining mental effort. He will go through periods where he makes great efforts in life, and low periods where he becomes depressed. He probably reacts to life rather than trying to create a comfortable personal lifestyle.

STRAIGHT LINES (Fig. 7.20)
It used to be said that mathematicians have straight head lines (a) while linguists have sloping ones and artistic people ultra sloping ones (b). That view is too restricted, but it does make sense. If the line runs straight across the hand, the person thinks in black and white; look at the second phalange of the thumb to see whether it is long for logical thinking or short for idiosyncratic

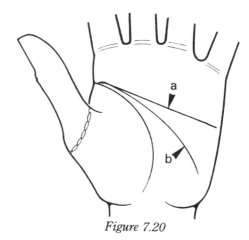

Figure 7.20

thinking. This subject prefers a practical career which offers security and normality. He could have problems in understanding or expressing feelings because, in addition to the lack of imagination shown by a long straight head line going into upper Mars (aggressive attitude), the emotional areas of Neptune/Luna and the heart line area are cut off from one another. A long straight line keeps this subject working to the end of his days because work offers him companionship, respect and self-respect plus a steady income. This is a team member rather than a boss.

THE LONG AND THE SHORT (Fig. 7.21)

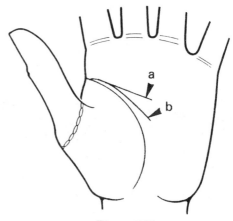

Figure 7.21

When the line is short and straight (a), there is deep concentration in a narrow field. This person could go far because his determined ambition coupled with his ability to focus on specific goals pushes him to the top. Malcolm has found this kind of line on the hand of a super civil servant who was very adept at filling up complicated forms. This lady could not see why Malcolm did not understand the required procedures.

This type likes to be in charge of others but, oddly enough, also needs the approbation of other people. (Check finger tips for whorls which would make more of a loner, loops for more sociability, and small, blue-coloured spatulate nails for tension and ambition.) This intense concentration may have nothing to do with work but could be poured into a particular hobby or interest. The only way to explain anything to this type is in terms of his own specialization; he will not understand anyone else's points of reference and will scoff at everything that is outside his own field of knowledge. We have tried to work out whether this type has a sense of humour or not, but we do not think he would find that funny.

THE SLOPING LINE
A short sloping line (Fig. 7.21b) belongs to the lazy thinker, someone who does not make much effort, does not want to learn and jumps from one idea to another.

THE DEGREE OF SLOPE
A slight slope brings a nice balance between practicality and imagination (a). This person has a mixture of interests and does not just live for work; he enjoys company and conversation. A steeper slope (b) belongs to someone who is able to understand people intuitively and may, therefore, work as a salesman, personnel officer or counsellor. There may be artistic or musical talents, a love of travel or of the countryside. If the slope is very steep (c), the imagination and intuition will be highly developed. A mother who has this kind of line would weave fabulous bedtime tales for her children but could also be temperamental and touchy. It is a double-edged sword as it endows talent and creativity but also moodiness, oversensitivity and, at least in childhood, fears and phobias. This slightly unworldly person needs to be alone from time to time, to meditate and retreat from the world. He has a tendency to sop up other people's sorrows, especially if there is also a girdle of Venus on the hand.

ENDINGS (Fig. 7.23)

If, in addition to a long head line, there is a

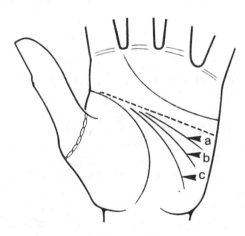

Figure 7.22

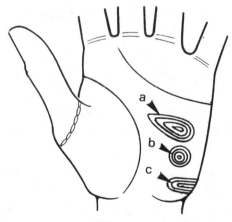

Figure 7.23

loop on Luna (a), the subject could have considerable success in some sort of creative work (see head line prints 7.29 and 7.30). He has a good memory which may help him in his work. A whorl on Luna (b) would add mediumistic tendencies, and a loop low on Pluto (c), or entering Luna from the percussion, would put him in tune with nature or the sea.

CREATIVE HEAD AND LIFE LINE (Fig. 7.24)

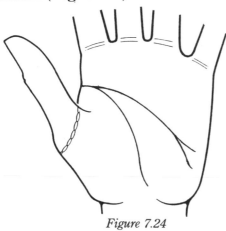

Figure 7.24

If the line runs parallel to a life line which also reaches out for Luna, there will be success as a writer or an artist. (NB In astrology Pluto and the Moon represent public success or influence and this seems to be backed up by palmistry!)

BRANCHES AND HOOKS — MAINLY UPWARDS (Fig. 7.25)

A head line which turns upwards (a) is not often seen but it shows success in business, probably at the expense of others. When the head and heart lines are close to each other (b) the emotions cloud the thinking; when they are widely spaced the person is calculating and could be a dangerous adversary.

Upward branches (c) are a form of mental self-help showing efforts to improve one's chances in life. Branches which are exceptionally strong, travelling directly towards

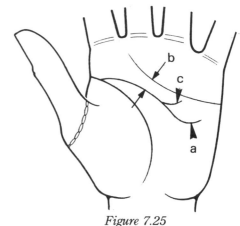

Figure 7.25

Mercury, *do* have a specific meaning because they show efforts to learn and communicate. They may also relate to business matters. Other upward branches have no specific meaning except to show times of effort. Even faint rising lines show attempts to rise above emotional or financial problems by studying, re-training, getting a better job, starting a business or just changing one's mental outlook. Downward branches might imply times of struggle and loss but are probably fork formations rather than branches. If a fork is as strong as the head line itself there would be an imaginative approach to communications which would inevitably be used in the subject's daily work. Traditionally this is called the 'writer's fork'. (Sasha has these on both hands as do all the other writers that we know.)

SIMIAN LINE, ESPECIALLY THE HEAD-LINE SIDE OF THIS LINE

This is a strong straight line which cuts across the hand (see Fig. 7.40) combining and compressing the normal head and heart line. Tradition has it that monkeys have this line, hence its name. Tradition also has it that people with Down's Syndrome have these lines. We have not seen any monkeys lately but we believe that their hands are actually much the same as ours. People who have Down's Syndrome **are no more likely to have simian lines than anyone else**.

About one person in fifteen has this kind of mark and it shows intense concentration, possibly obsession, regarding some part of their lives. They might get their feeling side and their thinking sides a bit mixed up, but they are not alone in that. There is tension shown here as feelings and emotions are held under heavy control and the two halves of the hands are separated by the line, causing the intuitive side (Neptune/Luna) to be parted from the affections and desires (heart line and mounts). Semi-simian lines also seem to put pressure on the emotions and may be associated with people who find it difficult to give love or to find someone who can love them. These people find it hard to concentrate on both work and relationships at the same time.

FORKS, MARKS AND ENDINGS (Fig. 7.26)

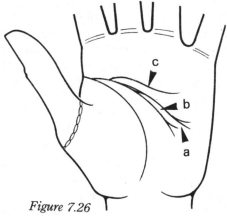

Figure 7.26

Tasselled endings (a) may show a lack of calcium, fluoride, potassium or just a great deal of worry. They may also indicate senile dementia; here one must look at the life line to see if that too is weak toward the southern end. A line which is clear and strong but ends in one or two splits (b) shows that the person will continue to work into old age but the work may be part-time,

voluntary or there may be many interests late in life. (Check with the top of the fate and Apollo lines.)

Heavily-forked, split or doubled head lines (c) have a number of meanings, all of which take some living with. The traditional meaning is of a split personality, a gentle form of schizophrenia. Certainly these people have plenty of talent — too many talents, in fact, as they can turn from practical to creative or intellectual pursuits and can cope with almost any situation as long as their nerves hold together. They sparkle with ideas, can work very hard and produce truly amazing things but they need rest and they also need to be attached to a steady, stable, plodding and untemperamental partner.

This person may have two parallel lives which allow him to explore two completely different facets of his personality. A good example would be of an accountant who was also a champion ballroom dancer; it is possible that his workmates would not even know of his hobby. This subject may chase too many rainbows and (especially if both hands have this formation) find it hard to finish a task without being diverted by something more interesting. Catch him on a good day and he can be more fun than a barrel load of monkeys, but on a bad day he will be angry and disappointed with himself. He has a good head for business too.

Islands, bars, breaks etc. all tell of health problems or setbacks in the course of life. A fairly common sign is that of an island with an effort line rising out of it. This shows a patch of worry, both practical and emotional, but the effort line shows us that the subject hauls himself out of the pit to make life worth living again.

Breaks in the line could show problems related to work but also illness and accident; a square covering a break will show the problem has been averted (see Chapter 11). Light squares indicate periods of frustration, of being bored and fed up with life in general and with one's job in particular.

The effort line shows that after a while the subject himself will find a more satisfying lifestyle.

CHAINED HEAD LINE
(Fig. 7.27)

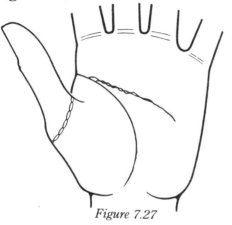

Figure 7.27

A chained line shows some kind of feeble-mindedness. This may range from an apathetic attitude to life and mental laziness to genuine mental handicap. Many small bars, or a patch of chaining, may indicate migraine, or a temporarily tense situation. Dots and bars also indicate migraine, possibly eye strain or other head and neck problems.

Some of us have hearts which appear to rule our heads but in reality it is the head line which rules every part of our lives. The line not only shows the picture of our capacity for learning and the way we think, but also how the nerves, emotions and energy rhythms (see Chapter 6) affect our mental outlook at different stages of our lives. The life line is very much linked with the head line — it is the root of its strength and energy; a long head line needs plenty of energy to keep it going.

REPEATED PATTERNS
(Fig. 7.7)

Many people's hands have characteristics such as islands and chained effects *appearing in an almost identical pattern on both the head and life lines*. It seems that these two lines radiate outwards from a central point where they are joined or are nearest to each other on the mount of lower Mars. A chained and islanded effect at the beginning shows a battle for energy between the brain and the body during the growing up period. This battle can go on for up to twenty-five years! The timing on the head line can be judged geometrically from the life line by looking closely at the illustration. (Fig. 7.7)

Roughly speaking the junction of the fate and head lines occurs at about thirty years of age, but if the head line is high on the hand, the fate line would cross it at approximately thirty-five years of age.

CASE HISTORY: JOHN
(Fig. 7.28)

This is the story of John, a young man who will pour his energies into work rather than make a success of his marriage. He will deny the emotional demands of his wife and family which make him feel uncomfortable, while pushing himself ahead in his career where he feels safe.

His head line slopes slightly but curls upwards in the latter stages suggesting a long journey toward ultimate career success. The long head line keeps him striving, becoming more business-like and goal-orientated as life goes on. The combination of that long, strong head line with a comparatively weak-looking life line shows a lack of balance in his life. There will be periods of depression and occasional feelings of failure because his desires (head) are not matched by his physical ability to achieve them (life). The tatty-looking ending to the head line with a small line reaching out from the percussion to grasp it (a) shows insomnia (see Chapter 12). The life line is intertwined with other lines which impede its progress. The difference between a smooth clear life line and one which has other lines wrapping themselves up with it is comparable to the difference in driving seventy miles along a motorway and seventy miles along a cart track.

The heavy line of restriction (b) belongs to a subject whose parents are extraordinarily repressive, who believe in some kind of emotionally restrictive 'hell fire' religion or are the type to insist on an arranged marriage. In the case of John, his parents were repressive and demanding and certainly did push him into a 'suitable' marriage.

An island tucked well into the middle of the life line (c) is evidence of emotional depression and unhappiness; in this case, at about twenty-two years. When a fate line remains tied to the life line along so much of its path (d), the parents continue to exert an influence over the subject in his early twenties when it is no longer appropriate.

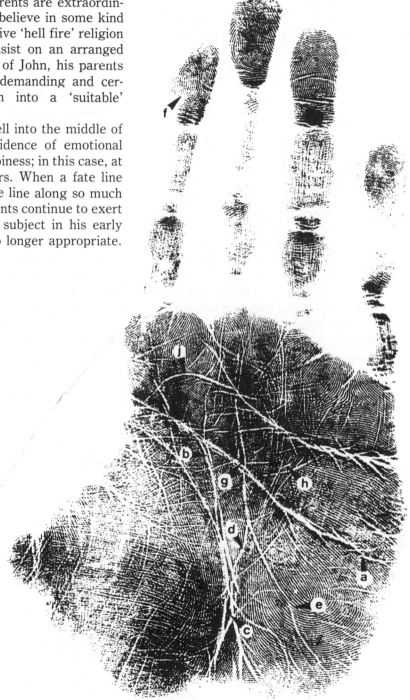

Figure 7.28

In John's case, there is a break in the fate line and also an alteration of its course (e) when his depression begins to interfere seriously with his work; notice the inclining short Jupiter finger (f). At that time he was totally unsure of his direction in life, probably due to the fact that until then his parents had taken his decisions for him. At the time of the reading his hands were too soft for a healthy young man, showing lack of energy.

His mental and emotional problems are not over yet. At the point where he is aged thirty-five an island appears on both the head and fate lines (g), there is also a relationship or marriage split V in the Apollo line (h). Any V which appears in the centre of the hand on the Apollo line will show marriage difficulties. This is followed by an energy rhythm at 38-40 years, lots of 'searching lines'. The head line is relatively clear at this point; therefore he will put his energies into work. The line from the heart line (j) is a safety valve. He will be able to channel his excessive nervous and emotional energies into work.

It appears, as things stand at the moment, that he will continue to do his duty to his wife and family and will make tremendous achievements in his career as a form of compensation. In addition to this compensatory factor, one can only speculate as to how much of this achievement is an unconscious and continuing desire to please and impress overcritical and overdemanding parents. How far would he be prepared to push himself if he were happily married? Will he, once he becomes rich and successful, become vulnerable to someone who appears to offer the opportunity to fill in the gaps in his sexual and emotional experience? Can we change the scenario to allow him to fall in love with a genuinely lovely woman and make a fresh start for himself? We cannot see any of these alternatives yet; but he is young, his character is still unformed, lines will change. His life story does not have to be so depressing, but it may be necessarily so in order to provide us with a truly memorable captain of industry.

A Quartet of Living Head Lines

RONALD (Fig. 7.29)

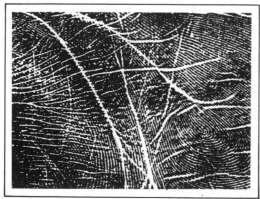

Figure 7.29

Ronald has a curved, imaginative head line which curls upwards toward the mount of Mercury. This shows that he will be a clever businessman with the ability to visualize the way to achieve results. The life line shows abundant energy, and the clear fate line shows mental alertness and a sense of purpose. The loop formation on Luna near the end of the head line shows a pool of imaginative energies from which he can draw. Because the head line reaches down to this pool, he can use it to bring artistic, creative and unusual methods of thinking to his work but the drawback is that he overthinks problems and finds it difficult to separate his business interests from the emotional side of his life. He may consider business problems from too emotional a standpoint.

At the age of twenty-seven the fate line forks and a decision line from Venus creates a blockage, thereby forcing him to make decisions and changes. Some of this is emotional. The fate line starts up again but it has jumped toward the ulna side which shows that his new beginning is something of a backwards step — his thinking is not as good as before.

JOANNA (Fig. 7.30)

Figure 7.30

Joanna has a straight practical head line which means that she likes her decisions to be clear-cut, black and white; hence also the strong and determined fate line. These features are 'fuelled' by a strong life line which shows that she will make a success of her career. She has two loop formations on Luna representing two pools of creative energy; this would point to the need for a creative element to her career.

Joanna is, in fact, a qualified hairdresser with the ability to visualize a finished hairstyle plus the practicality to create it. The mount of Neptune is quite high which links the imaginative Luna to the practical acquisitive, value-conscious Venus. She will go far.

PAUL (Fig. 7.31)

Paul has a crazily-split head line, which in this case does not imply brain damage because all the lines are joined at one point or another along their length. It means that Paul will start a job, become distracted, start another and forget to finish the first. As he is in a position of some authority, one can imagine the confusion which he leaves

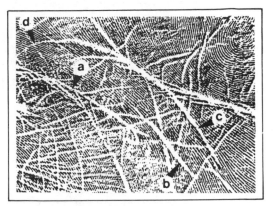

Figure 7.31

in his wake. Paul's head line is tied to the life line (a), showing early sensitivity and reluctance to relinquish the state of childhood and his ties to his parents. The middle section (b) is where you would expect to find the practical side of the head line; this section has a v formation which shows him to be unable to take decisions, preferring others to take them for him.

The third section (c) goes into the heart line and then curves over back to the head line. He is unsure of where his emotions lie. When part of the heart line goes into the head line (d) there is an uncertainty as to just what sex the subject feels himself to be. In Paul's case, he is married to the matronly type who keeps him in line. It seems that after reaching a reluctant adulthood, Paul has replaced his mother with a dominant mother-type figure.

MICHAEL (Fig. 7.32)

Michael's head line is too strongly tied to his life line (a) showing excessive timidity and a pessimistic attitude to life. He gives up too easily. The head line wavers and bends upwards and downwards showing that he is indecisive, changeable. The fate line is used as part of the life line (b) showing restriction, but also showing that such energies he has will be channelled into work. The short head line with a strong life

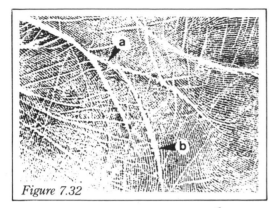
Figure 7.32

line of roughly the same length and appearance shows that he is mentally normal, albeit at the lower end of the scale. The shortness of the lines shows that he can only concentrate his efforts on one small area of life, in this case some kind of work. Michael will be virtually unable to make any normal social or emotional life for himself. He is just this side of being mentally handicapped.

The Heart Line

MALCOLM'S TALE

My first introduction to the value of palmistry was way back in my late teens. I went to a marriage guidance meeting with a girlfriend. The doctor giving the talk turned to the subject of 'what makes a good lover'. In my purity and innocence, I had not given it a thought. He said, 'The man with short fingers is too fussy and full of routine to become a good lover, but on the other hand,' he said, pointing at me, 'a man with long fingers is romantic and would make a good lover.' Needless to say, I promptly sat on my hands. Therefore, when looking at the heart line, look also at the *shape* of the hand.

BASIC INFORMATION

In the case of the head and life line it is best to have a clean clear line but a super-clear heart line would belong to someone inhuman. It is true that islands, breaks and bars indicate troubles but some of the other markings are very helpful.

THE HEART LINE IN SECTIONS (Fig. 7.33)

The heart line can be divided into three sections as follows:

(a) Heart line of the affections.
(b) Sensitivity.
(c) Heart and lungs.

There *are* health indications to be seen on

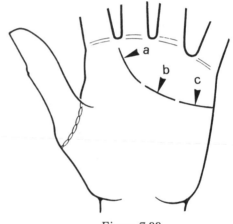
Figure 7.33

the heart line as a whole but section (c) is *mainly* concerned with health.

WHICH END OF THE LINE IS THE BEGINNING?

We have decided to call the percussion edge of the heart line the beginning. This is because the head and life line both start at the thickest point so it makes sense for the heart line to do so too. Events cannot really be dated by their position on the heart line. Therefore, if you see a trauma mark on the heart line please check the fate, Apollo and life lines — even the head line for corroboration and dating.

HEART LINE OF THE AFFECTIONS (a)

This part of the heart line is on the radial, active side, of the hand. It is how we give and receive love and it shows our attitude to sex and the part it plays in our life; the way we show and express ourselves to others and to the outside world. It might be a good idea to think of that part of the line as a hand reaching out for affection. Branches bring more feeling and receptivity, few branches mean pre-set views. A single line shows single mindedness as lots of lines suggest a reaching out and searching for something which may not exist.

Look at the quality of the line; a wispy line, barely on the skin, shows sexual unfulfilment; a dark patch of skin under the line shows anguish or depression over the emotional side of life.

CURVED HEART LINE (Fig. 7.34)

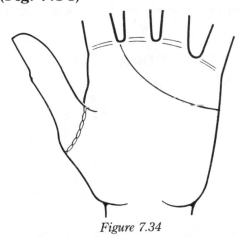

Figure 7.34

Curved lines show emotion, straight lines show control. A curved heart line belongs to a person who wants to relate; he is warm hearted and highly-sexed. A combination of a long, curved heart line and head line shows a good memory for emotional matters. This person will remember both the good times and the pain of past emotional experiences. Curved-line people are more open emotionally; they do not expect to find envy, spite or domination in a relationship, and they do not set out deliberately to hurt others.

STRAIGHT HEART LINE (Fig. 7.35)

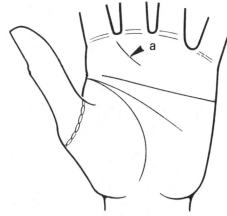

Figure 7.35

This person is emotionally controlled. If the line is exceptionally straight, he may be seeking perfection in relationships (good luck to him!). These people operate well on a level of friendship but less so in close personal relationships because they become upset if confronted with deep feelings. They complain that their partner does not care enough for them, but they themselves keep others at arms length — possibly without quite realizing what they are doing.

STRAIGHT HEART LINE WITH A WHOLE OR PARTIAL GIRDLE OF VENUS (Fig. 7.35)

Quite often one sees a straight line with all or part of the girdle of Venus above it (a); this shows sensitivity. This person could be putting some kind of fence around his feelings in order to protect them, and on the other hand he is *able* to feel his own pain, even if he still has trouble relating to the pain of others. At least he has the potential to become warmer-hearted and a better lover.

STRAIGHT HEART LINE ENDING ON LOWER JUPITER (Fig. 7.36a)

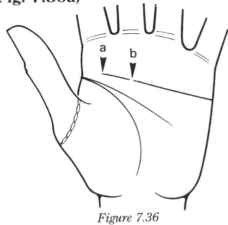

Figure 7.36

This shows a more mental type of loving. These people have to feel proud of their partners; they love them for having the 'right appearance', for their career or position in life, their religious or cultural suitability or their financial prospects. The actual personality of the partner is always secondary. This person, having chosen an 'acceptable' mate, then proceeds to become a fantasizer with a strongly romantic and receptive nature — even if only in his dreams. This is even more likely if there is a long, curved head line.

The heart line in this position can have an interesting practical application in that this person will have a very caring attitude toward people who are outside the immediate family. Their sexual energy and expression are frequently spent on their work. They seem to make their careers in nursing, teaching and social work, particularly if they have healing or medical striata. Someone with a straight heart line does not need a constant display of affection. Our friend Sheila McGuirk has noticed that these people are frequently seen to have a strongly marked Solomon's ring or 'caring line' which seems to imply that they are happiest when expressing love in a practical way for the community in general,

whilst feeling less comfortable in personal relationships. This kind of formation is also seen on the hands of rather paternal businessmen who 'look after' the interests of their staff.

STRAIGHT HEART LINE ENDING UNDER SATURN (Fig. 7.36b)

This short heart line belongs to a person who can withdraw into himself. When Malcolm was in America he saw a lady in her sixties who had a heart line like this and he suggested that although she had been married three times, she still asked the question, 'What is this thing called love?' She replied 'Do you know, that's my biggest secret — I have never found the answer.' The heart line in this position is the mental type of love. Love becomes sex with sensuality and no finesse. In a woman's hand there is a shrewd calculated approach to relationships. There might be lesbianism here — but all the emotions and sexual expression are held back for fear of ridicule or rejection.

ENDING UNDER SATURN (Fig. 7.37)

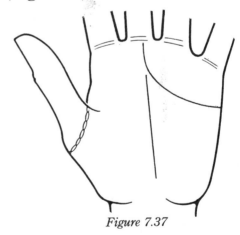

Figure 7.37

This line goes back to the self, so it displays a selfish outlook. The person is cold, not easily carried away emotionally, and the emotions are governed by sensuality. If the heart line is joined by the fate line the subject's heart may be poured into his work or pastimes. There may be a stifling of romantic and sexual feelings possibly caused by latent bisexuality, lesbianism or homosexuality. A cheerful homosexual with no hang-ups has a much more ordinary looking heart line but with a scimitar shaped hook downwards into the area where the head and life line join.

ENDING BETWEEN JUPITER AND SATURN (Fig. 7.38)

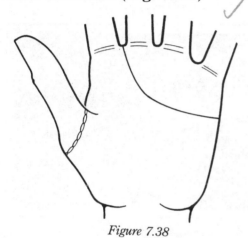

Figure 7.38

If this line is single, with few branches and no chaining, plus a vigorous curve, the sexual energy flows freely, therefore it is physical, instinctive, passionate and demanding. It is 'masculine' in nature and possibly leads to a rather selfish attitude to sex with little discussion of mutual needs because the subject considers that actions speak louder than words.

ENDING BETWEEN JUPITER AND SATURN BUT WITH A GENTLER CURVE (Fig. 7.39a)

A line like this with branches gives warm-heartedness and balance between the mind and the emotions. If the line travels tightly upwards between the fingers, love will be blind — the subject will see no wrong in the partner. If the heart line ends in a single line, there could be a single-minded atti-

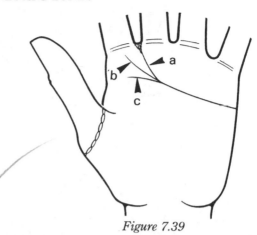

Figure 7.39

tude. The subject will be rather possessive and have an idealistic idea of love.

ENDING ON JUPITER (Fig. 7.39b)

This is where the character of the mount of Jupiter comes into play. There is idealism, ambition and egotism; if the heart line touches the base of the finger there will be jealousy and possessiveness. (NB If the heart line reaches the top of the palm at any point there will be a possessive streak.) If the line is strong, single and gently curved the subject may be a 'Don Juan' type who boasts about his sexual conquests but whose activities take place mainly in his imagination. He wants to make love without a hair out of place; he needs to keep his wristwatch on so that he does not feel totally denuded (he may even keep his socks on.) If these people cannot unbend, the sexual energy goes into ambition, especially if the fate line goes into the heart line and there is a strong Jupiter finger. If there is a branch line going into the lower part of Jupiter, (b and c) they will be more open, down to earth and will have a more caring attitude to others.

SIMIAN LINE (Fig. 7.40)

We have already dealt with this in the section on the head line (see page 82) but we would like to mention it here in connection with the *emotions*.

These people can only concentrate on one

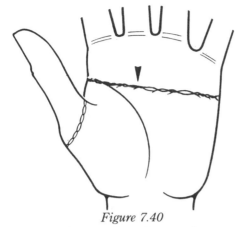

Figure 7.40

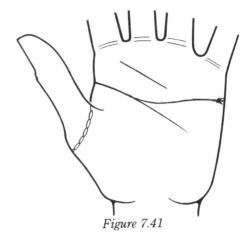

Figure 7.41

thing at a time so there is a tendency to be overbearing. They enter wholeheartedly into whatever they do and switch off all else. When it comes to love and the emotions, this singlemindedness is hard to live with unless one enters the relationship with the same intensity. It is hard for a person with this line to understand the feelings of others. They can swamp their partner with love which may be jealously emotional, born of insecurity and lack of confidence. Sometimes they feel love is a sign of weakness, and show remorse in violent unpredictable suspicion and inquisitions because they feel entombed within themselves.

If the subject is aware of his nature and tries to become more receptive to others, another heart line will begin to develop, probably the curve under Jupiter and Saturn, and this will put him in touch with both his own feelings and those of others. Sometimes the girdle of Venus becomes strong enough to be an infant heart line and this serves the purpose.

SEMI-SIMIANS AND OTHER ODD EFFECTS (Fig. 7.41 and 7.42)

Semi-simian lines show sociosexual hangups. These people are either so shy that they find it hard to talk personally to anyone, or they may be openly or latently homosexual and have suffered some sort of

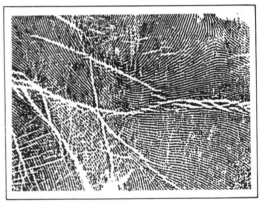

Figure 7.42

confusion over this. The confusion may result from their having to explain to their family why they are not going to marry and produce grandchildren. There may be other fears and phobias related to childhood experience (we even came across one client with this kind of formation who had been the victim of incest). Other screwed-up characters seem to get their kicks only from work and not in relating at all, and yet others seem to be totally in love with their car or completely absorbed in the complexities of their central-heating system.

CENTRE SECTION OF THE HEART LINE (Fig. 7.43a and b)

This section concerns sensitivity, and it is apt to change its appearance very quickly as it reveals how the subject feels at any one time.

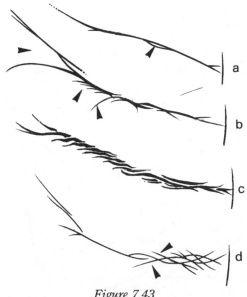

Figure 7.43
Centre Section of Heart Line

FIG. 7.43a
If there is a single heart line with no branches, the subject will have a tight hold on his emotions and want to be in control at all times. These people like the emotional side of life to be straightforward and find it hard to understand that it takes two to make a relationship. Love to them is a form of loyalty; sex is an urge that has to be gratified. If they have any emotional difficulty or shock it shows up as an island or a number of islands, in the central section of the line.

FIG. 7.43b
Same type of line as above but more sensitive, volatile, insecure, these people have their ups and downs and hurts in emotions. Short, curved branches falling below the line are flirtation lines. Long, downward-curved branches represent emotional disappointments. Branches at the 'affection' end of the heart line give warmth and idealism, passion and a sensible approach to relationships and to other people. This is the area where you find friendships. A couple of strong lines curving downwards here show deep abiding friendships. They look a little like the drooping line which indicates homosexuality and to some extent come from the same source, because friendships are invariably with one's own sex and they serve as great a need in a heterosexual person's life as do love relationships.

TAKE THESE CHAINS FROM MY HEART AND SET ME FREE (Fig. 7.43c and d)
This line from a pop song is quite apt because chains show unfulfilment and unhappiness. If severe, there could be cruelty and victimization within a relationship.

FIG. 7.43c
A woven type of heart line shows sensitivity brought about by mineral deficiencies in the diet. This can also show depression. The subject needs to calm down because he or she is hypersensitive.

FIG. 7.43d
Look at this heart line in its entirety but only at the sensitivity aspect. Here we have a spiky 'thorny' looking line under Mercury. When the spikes face inwards toward the palm, the subjects are emotionally spiky. They may be kicking out against childhood days as if they were still haunted by unhappy early emotional experiences. There is also a self-persecution aspect.

BREAKS IN THE LINE (Fig. 7.44)
A break in the line just where it begins to curve upwards (a) seems to show the sudden ending of a relationship. This may be due to sudden divorce or death. Look also for a deletion line near the end of an attachment line, plus a spinster line. If there is an isolated island on this section, the spouse might be seriously ill. If the line continues cleanly after the island and/or there is an effort line rising up from the heart line, the spouse will recover completely.

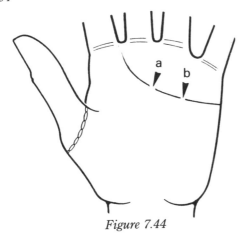

Figure 7.44

Our friend John tells us that a clean break between the Mercury and Apollo area (b) shows celibacy, as in the case of a Catholic priest, or a separation of love relationships and sexual ones. Sasha remembers hearing an elderly lady speaking on television about her life who remarked that she had always had more than one man in her life as she never seemed to 'find love and sex in the same shop'. Although we can not corroborate this, we feel certain she had this kind of 'snap' in the line.

LINES WHICH FIRMLY JOIN THE HEART LINE TO THE HEAD LINE (Fig. 7.45)

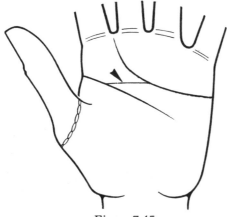

Figure 7.45

A line which firmly joins the heart line to the head line shows a marriage of non-communication. If there are two of these, the subject may have left one non-relater only to find another!

DOUBLE HEART-LINES (Fig. 7.46)

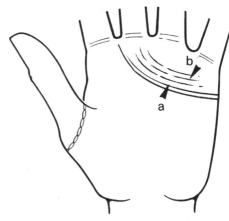

Figure 7.46

(a) These are supposed to be a sign of deep loyalty. They suggest an amorous nature and tremendous devotion in love. An extra line here strengthens the heart line in the same way that the line of Mars aids the life line. Double heart lines also make for a lively and animated personality.

(b) A 'shadow' of the heart line, with fragments repeated above the line, show some form of other loyalty. We have seen this in the case of people who have re-married and have almost completely cut themselves off from their previous family, but the feelings, especially for the children, still linger.

INFLUENCE LINES (Fig. 7.47)

(a) Good ones: These come from under the heart line and join it. They can indicate useful friendships or rather caring business partners.

(b) Bad ones: These come from within the life line. They can be termed family aggravation lines and they show that the family is interfering in the subject's relationships in some way.

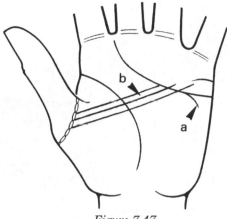

Figure 7.47

DETERMINING THE POSITION OF THE LINE (Fig. 7.48)

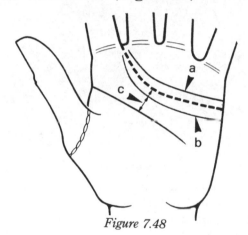

Figure 7.48

(a) If the heart line is close to the fingers, it suggests an intellectual approach to love and the emotions. This person is rational, analytical and cool. The head rules the heart.

(b) A deeply curved heart line low on the palm with podgy mounts is the gushing sympathetic type who pours out love in order to help others. A gradual curve shows that the heart rules the head, especially if there is a star near the end of the head line on Luna.

(c) If the heart line is close to the head line, the subject is narrow minded; a broad space between the lines suggests someone who is broad minded.

It is also worth noting that people who have curved heart lines are more domesticated and home-loving on the whole than the people with straight lines, who are probably more career-minded.

OTHER MARKS

Crosses and bars are setbacks and interference of some kind. Discoloured, faded, smudgy, whitish or glassy patches show periods of trouble, illness or depression over personal relationships. These will clear away as the problem passes away.

A Quartet of Heart Lines

KAREN — DETACHED HEART LINE (Fig. 7.49)

The first impression given by this line makes one think of heart trouble because it stops short on the ulna side of the hand, but the lower 'semi-simian' line acts as a replacement for the missing part of the heart line. This type of line is found on the hands of warm-hearted people and the humour loop resting on this line makes this attractive young lady delightful to be with. The doubled heart line indicates loyalty and the semi-simian indicates shyness: this

Figure 7.49

young woman desperately wants a boyfriend but is unable to bring herself out to
face the emotional side of life.

This set-up is typical of people who are
unsure of themselves sexually and unsure
of exactly what they need and how to get it.
They are happy to relate as a friend but find
the emotional side nerveracking. They
need a strong, comfortable, loving, caring
partner.

Figure 7.51

JACKIE — GIRDLE OF VENUS PUSHING DOWN THE HEART LINE (Fig. 7.50)

Figure 7.50

In this hand all of the major lines are
chained, making the subject feel as if she
herself is in chains. The amount of emotional energy produced in this person's
body is more than the head line can cope
with. At the age of sixteen she showed a
tendency toward hysteria and depression,
also nymphomania. She has since spent her
life in and out of institutions.

JASON — STRAIGHT HEART LINE (Fig. 7.51)

This is not a simian line because of the
separate head line. A little embryo heart
line gives a certain balance. See the section
on straight heart-lines (page 89) for details.

TERRY — STRAIGHT AND TIGHT (Fig. 7.52)

Terry is a businessman whose wife died in

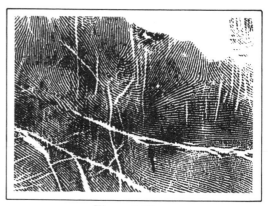

Figure 7.52

an accident in a car which he was driving.
Note the island in the sensitive section of
the heart line indicating a terrible emotional shock. The relationship lines on
Venus stop at the age point when the accident occurred and a dot marks the place.

DOUBLED LINES

These show split energies according to the
line involved. Double fate or head line
shows there could be two parallel careers.
If the heart line is doubled, there could be a
peculiar way of relating to others — a
person, for instance, who blows hot and
cold, who wants to be loved but rejects the
lover. A doubled life line suggests there
could be two separate issues which take up
the subject's time. The idea behind this
doubling is either that of double duties or of
a schizophrenic way of looking at life.

CHAPTER EIGHT

A New Way of Looking at Lines

This is where our book differs radically from previous hand-reading books. We have already introduced the reader to new concepts such as realistic hand shapes and energy rhythms but the following drawings and ideas are so different that they may appear confusing at first glance. We suggest that you take this section bit by bit, taking a long look at your friends' hands and checking their experiences against our findings until you feel completely at home with our concepts.

We would like to see our readers looking at the hand as a whole rather than taking a line by line analysis. We want you to be like an art critic studying a new painting, who would look first at the whole picture and then examine it in block segments. It may look complicated, but you will soon get the hang of it!

How to Read Events in the Hand

This section brings together all the previous chapters because while you are reading from one area of the hand, you will need to modify your conclusions by constant reference to other characteristics found on the hands. For instance, if there is strong evidence that your subject is going to look after sick or elderly parents, take into consideration whether he (or she) has the type of personality capable of doing this. Positive indications would be a rounded (conic) hand, a line of Solomon, 'waisted' thumbs and fingers, curving heart line, sloping head line, fingers that space slightly, Jupiter finger curving slightly towards Saturn etc. Negative indications would be a heavy square hand with whorls on the fingers, a Jupiter finger which bends sharply outwards, a heavy thumb, straight head line, high mounts of Venus, Jupiter and Mars — this subject would get his or her partner to do it!

Remember that the dominant hand is reality; the minor hand is the 'I wish' hand (see Chapter 1). All this is going to take practice but it has a logical basis even if it appears a little obscure at first. Just remember this simple rule: vertical lines which travel toward the radial side indicate improvement, motivation, action. Lines which travel toward the ulna side show inner achievement, homely pleasures and successes, sometimes setbacks if on the fate line.

It is essential to bear in mind the meaning and characteristic of each line and the direction it is taking. Remember the meaning of the mounts or areas of the hand. We have divided the hand into three horizontal zones which, for clarity, we have termed lower, middle and upper zone, and we have started our analysis at the lower zone.

LOWER ZONE — CHILDHOOD TO APPROXIMATELY THIRTY YEARS

The earliest experiences of life are drawn deeply into the psyche and can affect our behaviour and motivation ever after. We are all familiar with the type of person who, having been brought up in extreme poverty, fights his way to success and riches. How much of this energy and ambition is part of his nature and how much of it is due to his early environment? This is the crux of the 'nature or nurture' argument and also Jung's theory of the collective unconscious and unconscious ancestral memories.

LOWER ZONE — LIFE LINE ARCHING OUTWARDS INTO THE PALM (Fig. 8.1A)

When the line is continuous and it arcs outwards toward the palm, there is a balance between the inner needs and worldly achievement. These people need love and family life as well as a career. They have a reasonably adventurous nature; they enjoy travel, meeting new people and take an interest in the world about them. They seek a secure and sensible home life and probably want more for themselves and their children than their parents were able to provide.

LIFE LINE CLINGING ROUND VENUS (Fig. 8.1B)

This person needs *inner* satisfaction. He is a good relater, he needs a partner to love.

Work is secondary unless it gives strong *inner* satisfaction, such as art, music, craftsmanship. Not being very adventurous, he gains most of his pleasures from quite homely pursuits; he may have a beautiful garden, for instance. He either wants to repeat the kind of home life his parents provided or just falls into their way of doing things.

LIFE LINE REACHING OUT INTO LUNA (Fig. 8.1C)

Eventually work will become more important to this subject than home; he will put his energies into getting on. His spirit is adventurous and he may feel stifled by the home atmosphere. He is interested in the world outside and will want to leave an impression on it. He will strive for a better or different standard of living from that of his parents and may move geographically a long distance from the place of his birth. If there is no great geographic move, then look for a dramatic difference in aspirations.

A wife may develop a totally different outlook from her husband during the course of marriage, especially if the marriage took place early in life. There could be a strong reaction against childhood poverty — 'I'll never wear cast offs again' — or cultural poverty — 'no one read a book or listened to music in my parent's house' — or emotional poverty — 'all he wanted from me was to provide him with babies and clean the kitchen floor while he went out and had a good time'.

LIFE LINE SPLITS AT THE SOUTHERN END (see also Fig. 7.2)

The subject's energies are split. This could be a medical condition (check with upper zone and Chapter 12 on health). There could be a split in the subject's inner needs which fluctuate between wanting to concentrate on the emotional side and the career side of life. When the life line is split yet the the two forks are close together with no fate line on the lower zone, life is seen as a struggle, it is a matter of survival.

A typical case would be that of a single parent bringing up a child.

Lower Zone

FATE LINE
When reading the fate line in this zone, the life line will represent the parents and home.

NO FATE LINE
The subject has no particular ambition at this stage. He may be held back by powerful parents or life may be just too comfort-

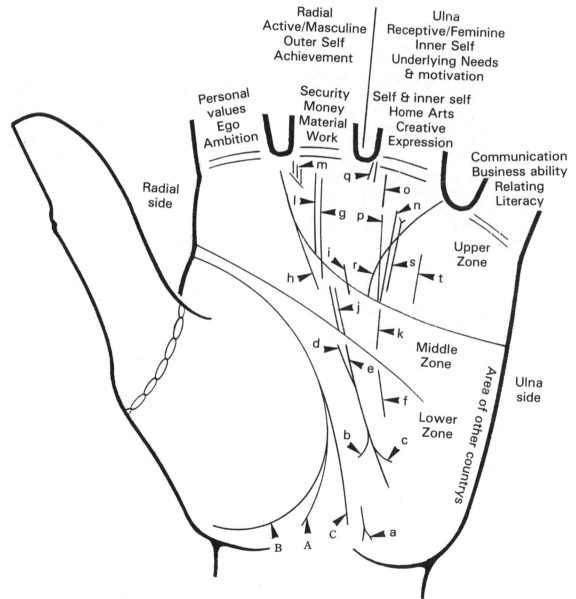

Figure 8.1 Events in the hand and map of the palm

able at home for him to want to strike out on his own. He may be drifting along or living in a protected environment such as the services, or even in borstal or prison. If there is mental illness, there might be a brownish stain colour on the skin.

This person is not, at least in his youth, a self-starter; he might have to wait for his courage to develop or for a change of circumstances to stir him up.

FATE LINE PART OF LIFE LINE

First check that this is not a split life line, which has a different meaning.

Restricted early in life, this subject may be held back by his parents or he could work in the family business. This could turn out to be a useful start for him if he develops ambition later on; a long or thick Jupiter finger and a strong-looking thumb would provide an instant clue. Even though this might hamper him, he could be grateful for a job when jobs are hard to find — having a **fate line** implies some sense of **responsibility**.

FATE LINE BEGINS APART FROM LIFE LINE

This shows independence, leaving home early. If there are lines connecting the fate line to the life line, the subject will keep in touch with his parents and will return from time to time. The greater the distance between the fate and life lines, the greater the distance, mentally and physically, from the parental home. This is an independent and self-reliant young person. A line which breaks and overlaps on the ulna side means that the subject will move further away from his childhood home town.

FATE LINE BEGINNING ON THE INSIDE OF THE LIFE LINE, ON THE MOUNT OF VENUS

This person is dictated to by his family. His career and personal life are ruled by them and he is unable to liberate himself — or maybe he prefers it that way.

LINES WHICH RUN INTO AND JOIN THE FATE LINE (Fig. 8.1)

(a) A subject who has these joining lines very low down on the palm will be physically and mentally ready for a serious relationship, such as marriage, when still very young. The age can be determined by the point at which the line enters the fate line (see Chapter 6). If a subject marries at some age before there are any joining lines, he may not be ready for such a relationship, which could cause problems later.

(b) A line which enters the fate line from the radial side indicates meeting a partner through work or through one's parents.

(c) A line entering from the ulna side shows that the partner is chosen from the world outside and away from the influence of parents and workmates. This person also makes an impression on people outside the family and looks for work that offers changes of scenery. A long line entering the fate line indicates a long relationship before marriage. The hands, of course, only register *emotional* commitment, not ceremonies or certificates.

A fine line from the ulna side could indicate help and training at work.

NO LINES ENTERING THE FATE LINE

It is quite possible for a person to be married with no lines entering the fate line. The marriage will be for convenience, a suitable arrangement all round — love, it is hoped, will come later.

Y-SHAPED SPLIT IN FATE LINE

This indicates change of direction, a new beginning — could be home, job, relationship, anything.

FIG. 8.1d

If the split line on the radial side stops, the material and career side of life will take a back seat while the domestic and emotional side develop, such as when a young woman gives up work to have children.

FIG. 8.1e

If the branch line on the ulna side stops, career, money and ambition will become important while the emotional side is left for the time being.

NO APOLLO LINE

The home is temporary; the subject could be moving around in connection with his job, living in rented accommodation, not yet settled in a permanent home of his own.

CLEAR APOLLO LINE
(Fig. 8.1f)

The home should be well established early in life. The subject could make a profession in the arts or he could have a strong attachment to the area he grew up in.

TWO FATE LINES

Life seems to be out of phase — 'if I had done this, I could have done that' or 'if it wasn't for that, I could have done this'. There is always an element of regret.

CASE HISTORY: JANET (lower zone) (Fig. 8.2)

Janet married at nineteen (a). The marriage was full of difficulties, hence the series of islands. The large island shows the couple trying to come together; notice the lines (b) nearly touching, also a line entering the fate line (f) signifying a coming together.

Janet went back to her parents (c) (here the life line is used as parents). At the same time the split (d) with a decision line cutting across, plus an island on the life line (g), shows a period of depression and unhappiness.

She will meet another man at age twenty-four to twenty-five, when a line (c) enters the fate line and changes the direction of the fate line toward Jupiter. Also the influence lines stop at twenty-five, so life becomes easier and she begins to take responsibility for her own life.

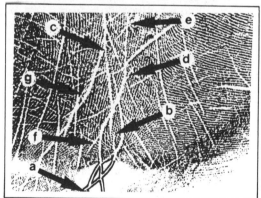

Figure 8.2

Middle Zone

Age approximately between thirty and forty years.

FATE LINE (Fig. 8.1g)

If it is travelling towards Saturn, work is for money not for job satisfaction.

FIG. 8.1h

If it joins the heart line, the heart will be put into work. NB A fate line which runs into the girdle of Venus means a workaholic.

SHORT EXTRA LINE BETWEEN FATE AND APOLLO (Fig. 8.1i)

This indicates starting a business or working from home.

FIG 8.1j
Where there are two parallel lines, energy is used to the full, the subject is fully stretched, he or she could be taking on too much. This could be due to running a small business or some kind of freelance work. Incidentally, this is a good indication on a young woman's hand that she will have children, as the pressure on her time and energy could come from working while bringing up children. (Other indications of motherhood would be small lines falling away from the life line on the mount of Venus side, possibly due to the physical strain of pregnancy; also children lines — see Chapter 9.)

APOLLO LINE (Fig. 8.1k)
Note how the lines begin to spread themselves outwards in this part of the hand. An Apollo line in this area of the hand indicates an emphasis on home, relationships and inner needs. If the Apollo line jumps, branches or leans to the ulna side the domestic and emotional side of life will be even more emphasized.

If the Apollo line seems to 'draw' fine lines away from the fate line in this area, the subject could work from home, or search strongly for self-expression and inner satisfaction in his work — this would point to the need for a creative outlet.

The meaning of some of the findings in the upper zone can relate to middle-zone matters. For instance, a person could start a business at any age, but this may only show in the upper zone.

Y-SHAPED SPLIT ON APOLLO
Same as on the fate line.

CASE HISTORY: THOMAS (middle zone) (Fig. 8.3)
Thomas is now forty-three and this story started when he was twenty-nine, therefore some of the earlier fine lines are now breaking up and fading. An islanded interference line (a) crosses the life line, cuts into the fate and Apollo lines and ends in a wart (b).

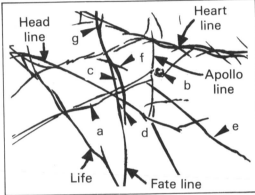

Figure 8.3

All this, especially the wart, indicates a time of great stress. An island on the fate line (c) shows that this period of stress affected the whole of his life at that time.

Thomas married at the age of twenty-nine, and later on had a casual affair with a woman he met at work. Note that at the beginning of the island (c), the lines run parallel: the closeness and then converging of the tiny line *inside* the island (d), coming from the ulna side but *inside* the island to touch the radial side, would indicate an affair with someone at work.

His in-laws got to hear of the affair, and forced him to act — note the decision line (a). This line is found on many hands and can be traced from the family line across the hand to just under the attachment lines on the ulna side; it shows marriage difficulties due to parents or in-laws interfering.

In order to prevent a full-scale scandal,

Thomas's company decided to send him to work in their West German branch (e). The 'split' or extra head line in this case travels outwards from the main influence line and the wart (b) — nature tends to grab the nearest line and utilize it in order to tell its story. As this line (e) goes to the area of travel and other countries at one end and stops at the interference line at the other with a long island (c), one can only deduce that his trip to Germany gave him time and space to think things out. If you extend this line (e) upwards to the fate line, it becomes another decision line (f). The couple come together here for a few years and then finally separate at the split (g), just under the heart line, when Thomas was thirty-eight.

Upper Zone

Life from age approximately forty onwards. This zone is most important because the findings here can be projected back to the other two zones, as the lifestyle projected here has its roots in the events of the lower two zones.

LACK OF LINES
On an empty hand one must search carefully for lines under the skin. If there is a blank area above the fate and Apollo lines, there will be a drop in the energies; the subject could become ill or just give up on life, allowing a kind of lethargy to set in. One must look for medical problems which may show up on the life and heart lines. On a more mundane level, there may be financial loss or the loss of a relationship causing material and emotional hardship.

FATE LINE (Fig. 8.1g)
One line to Saturn shows single mindedness, also a secure and unchanging life, e.g. remaining in the same job for years with a secure and regular income. A fine supplementary line on the ulna side of the fate line indicates a supplementary income, a second job.

TWO PARALLEL LINES (Fig. 8.1g and l)
These indicate freelance work, self-employment, having to turn one's hands to anything, or struggling with a very difficult job and a lot of responsibility.

MANY STRONG LINES
Many lines around the fate line indicate that finances are being stretched. If there is a large blank area to the north, the subject may overdo things and develop health problems as a result. Another outcome may be that he cannot win the battle against mounting losses and finds himself broke, bankrupt etc. A secondary fate line going toward Apollo shows a new kind of job which would be based in or around the home.

A secondary fate line which reaches toward the Apollo finger shows inherited money.

MANY FINE LINES
This could indicate a drink or drug problem. The subject may just be searching for a better way of life or he could be a dabbler in business, a generally inconsistent type of person. As seen in Fig. 8.1m this could indicate lending money to others and/or keeping busy in old age.

APOLLO LINE (Fig. 8.1n)
It is important, and sometimes rather difficult, to establish which line actually *is* the Apollo line here. It might be a good idea to push the hand away from you a bit in order to see which line stands out most. Note which line is the deepest or least broken up. Once you have established which is the Apollo line, take it to represent the subject's home base. If the line reaches

well down into the middle zone, he would live in the same area, probably the same house, for many years. If the line suddenly fades out and there is a blank area to the north, the subject could lose his home and possessions through financial disaster or marriage difficulties, it restricts him.

Lines which start again after a break (Fig. 8.1o) indicate a new home, a move or a fresh start, probably rather late in life. An island on this line means trouble through property or living in a 'jinxed' or unlucky house.

Y SHAPE AT THE TOP OF THE APOLLO LINE

A large split means living with a difficult person; a small split, living with someone whose health is poor or who is disabled or incapacitated. The partner would require extra help and attention but manages to lead as normal a life as possible with plenty of activities.

SPLIT APOLLO LINE (Fig. 8.1p)

This can mean a couple living together side by side with separate interests, co-existing rather than making a true relationship. A big split which starts at the heart line and which forms a slight hollow between the two splitting lines means that the subject has a long-term disability. Look also for a close split at the southern end of the life line.

LINES ON THE RADIAL SIDE OF APOLLO (Fig. 8.1p)

Fine lines, almost parallel, indicate a wish to move house which is *not* fulfilled; if the lines become stronger, the move may then take place. A line which merges with Apollo may indicate a second home bought as an investment.

TWO PARALLEL LINES AT THE TOP OF APOLLO (Fig. 8.1q)

This means living with someone in old age, possibly family or a friend. If the two lines lean toward one another or merge, this will be a love relationship. The lower end of the life line will also curve around the mount of Venus.

LINES ON THE RADIAL SIDE OF APOLLO (Fig. 8.1r)

These indicate hobbies, studies, work in the arts or work at home. This can also show that the subject works in or near the home in a counselling or healing capacity.

If the line reaches over toward the Mercury finger, it becomes most important as it shows that the subject is actively seeking out people with like minds, those who are on his wavelength. This can have a bearing on current and future relationships because these people develop interests that become part of themselves which lead them to associate with similar people.

These subjects may move ahead intellectually, socially or spiritually so quickly that they finally discover that they have very little in common with their current partner. A line here, close to Apollo, can also indicate a person who works with animals.

LINES ON THE ULNA SIDE OF APOLLO (Fig. 8.1s)

This side of Apollo concerns the people around or closely connected with the subject. The closer the lines are to Apollo, the closer the connection; the further away the greater the distance, either geographical or emotional. In this area of the hand one will find parents who need help; these subjects would look after parents until the end of their days. If there is a small blocking line where the line terminates, this is also the death of a loved one. However, if the line splits at the top, the person being taken care of will be disabled or incapacitated.

Another meaning to the same kind of line may be a close sexual relationship, possibly in addition to the marriage or Mother might come to tea and stay for years! Either way it indicates a need, and a desire, to put oneself out for someone other than the immediate family. A Y formation here shows an unhappy relationship. It can also show that the subject's affections are poured into caring for animals.

LINE PARALLEL TO APOLLO (Fig. 8.1t)
This outpost of Apollo shows love and duty at a distance. It may mean that the subject worries about his parents or some other person who lives at a distance. It could show life in two homes: to check this, look to see if there are also two family lines at the appropriate age of the placement. There may be a longing to put distance between the subject and his family, if they make him miserable; or just a longing to escape from one's responsibilities. If these lines join, there could be a marriage to a friend who lives far away.

How to trace events up the Fate and Apollo Line

CASE HISTORY: SAMUEL, A RETIRED FARMER (Fig. 8.4)
This print belongs to Sam, who is now aged sixty-three. He comes from a farming family and is himself a farmer.

Sam began his career by working for his father as shown by the fate line inside the life line (a). At approximately the age of twenty-three he got his own farm. The fact that there is actually a fate line hidden below the level of the skin before that age shows that for some years he had wanted to be independent. At the age of twenty-four he married (b). The fate line becomes stronger here and the two lines coming together show a union. There was an element of social pressure; it was correct to marry and have sons to carry on the tradition of the land. His wife is also shown on Venus (c), with a line from the family line forming showing a decision.

An effort line (d) with an island shows illness — in this case, lung trouble. (Lung or heart problems are shown by an island under Mercury or under the Apollo/Mercury junction.) This meant that it took considerable effort for him to get his farm going. In his thirties the fate line travels toward Jupiter showing an improvement in his business. When Sam was in his forties his father asked him to help out on his (father's) farm as he was becoming too frail to cope. A line from the family line (e) shows that he had to alter his life. The line on the radial side of the Apollo line shows him helping his father.

The line representing his parents ends (f) when his father dies; at this point Sam's age is forty-six years. He helped his mother to keep the farm going until she died (g) when Sam was fifty-two years old.

The line (h) from the family line where the two fate lines cross shows him bringing the two farms together into one unit. The line to Apollo also shows a legacy. His wife died when he was sixty-one years of age (i). Note how the line on Venus becomes light, also the shock island on the heart line (j). There is even a line from his marriage on Venus to this island. Now the lines are delving under the skin as he passes his farm on to his son.

Note also the strong teaching line and healing lines (k). He has always worked with cattle rather than cereals, using his ability to heal and care for living creatures. The teaching line shows that he is able to judge cattle at shows. Now he has retired, this is his main interest in life.

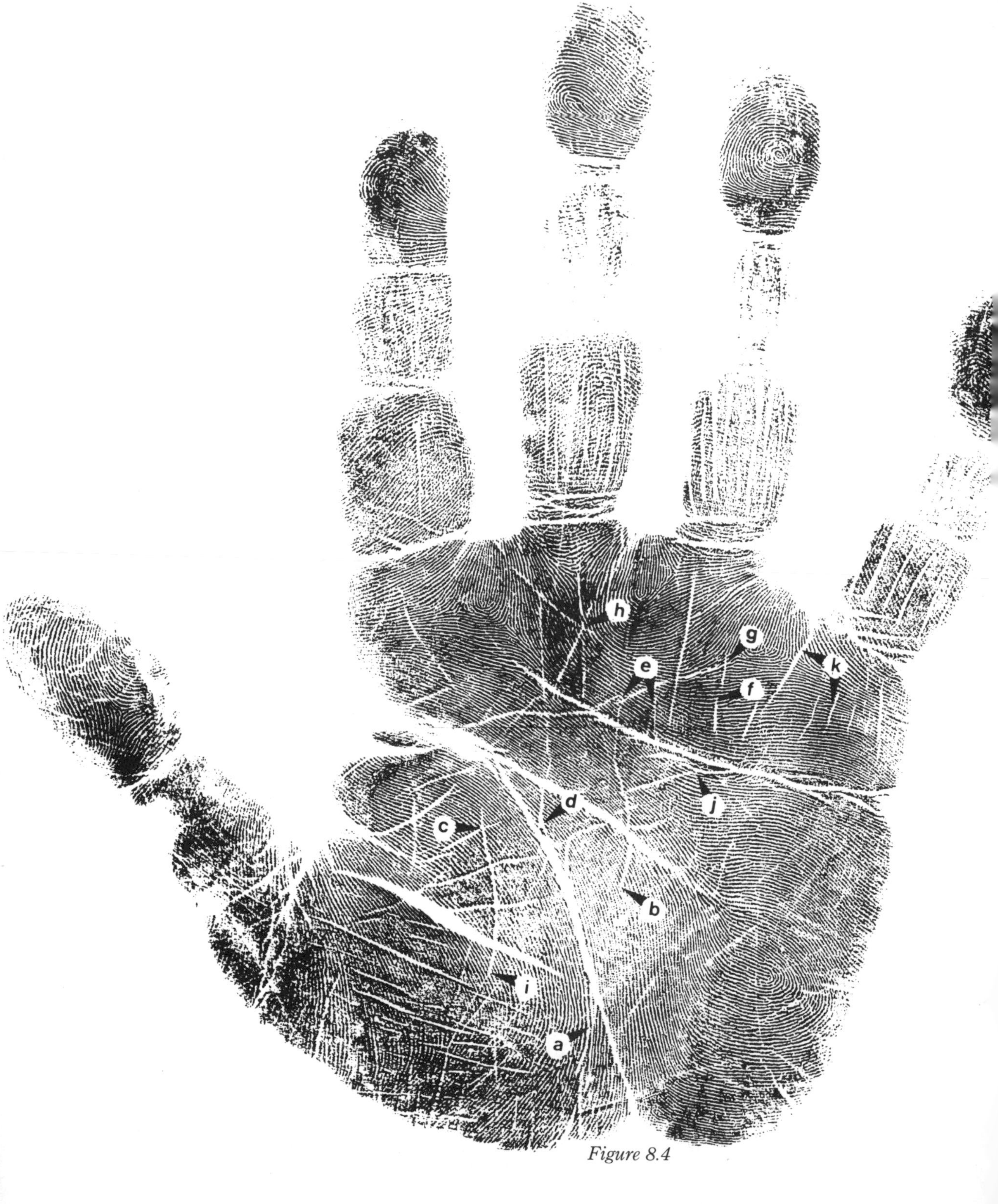

Figure 8.4

CHAPTER NINE

The Relating Lines:

Attachment, Child, Girdle of Venus, Sibling

The Attachment Lines

We call the small strong horizontal lines which enter the hand from the percussion side of the mount of Mercury 'attachment lines' because nowadays people may choose to live together in strong relationships without actually marrying. These lines give the palmist a good deal of information about the subject's attitude of mind (and body) to strong and close long-term emotional relationships.

ONE STRONG LINE

This should, all being well, indicate one steady relationship, probably marriage. If the line is bold and clear and the heart line is also clean and clear, this subject should enjoy a long and happy marriage. It is a real pleasure to see a hand like this as it is all too rare. This person marries with the intention of being totally faithful in body and loyal in mind to his or her partner. There is a supportive attitude to the spouse and the subject has the ability to overlook the occasional outburst or aggravating mood. There is little likelihood of this kind of marriage breaking up, but in the event of this occurring, the subject would marry again with the same intention of steady faithfulness.

From time to time we see this kind of hand on an elderly widow, and when we suggest that the marriage was a happy one, she agrees and may even be seen wiping away a tear or two. These elderly people truly miss their companion; they rarely re-marry but stay faithful to their partner's memory.

TWO STRONG LINES

These subjects usually marry more than once. This could be because they do not find the right partner the first time around, or question themselves as to the type of marriage they want, and decide against the one that they have. If their partner leaves, they usually marry again.

THREE OR MORE LINES

These people like relationships but need sexual freedom; this is especially true if there is a girdle of Venus which reaches across the hand to the mount of Mercury. This would make any really long-term relationship impossible unless there was a strong financial reason for making it work.

STRENGTH OF FEELINGS

Look on the percussion side of the hand toward the back of the hand. If two lines converge to make one attachment line, the feelings for the partner are very strong. If there is one line then there may be other reasons for the marriage or it may have been entered into rather lightly.

ONE STRAIGHT LINE (Fig. 9.1a)
This indicates one good marriage.

A LINE WHICH CURVES DOWN (Fig. 9.1b)
This shows disappointment in relationships which can lead to partings or divorce. The subject feels himself to be 'put upon' by the partner and may have to tolerate rather miserable circumstances in order to keep the peace.

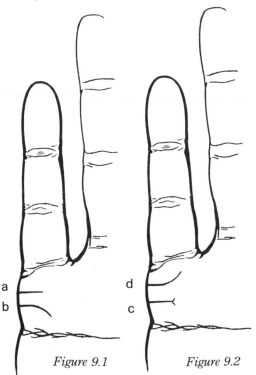

Figure 9.1   Figure 9.2

A STRAIGHT LINE WITH A SMALL FORK (Fig. 9.2c)
This signifies a sudden decision to end the marriage. A client of ours who had struggled through sixteen years of a really rotten marriage once said to us, 'One day a bell seemed to ring somewhere in my head

and I took myself off to see a solicitor. After discussing the formalities he asked me if I had any second thoughts. I found myself replying that I wished that I had had the courage to do this many years before.'

If practically the whole line is forked the subject is aware, albeit unconsciously, that the marriage has never been fulfilling. This can still lead to divorce but in a more leisurely fashion; when the children are grown up or there is enough money in the kitty to comfortably support two homes.

A LINE WHICH CURVES UPWARDS (Fig. 9.2d)
A line which can be seen curving upwards shows that the subject has a partner who will do well out in the world. The improvement in the spouse's income and status could be of great benefit to the client. If this is the case, the heart line will be clean and clear, the fate line smooth and aiming toward Jupiter, there will be an isolated cross high on Jupiter and their there will be no other strongly-marked attachment lines.

However, human nature being what it is, there can be friction and jealousy due to the change in their situation — especially if it is the woman who does well. If it is the man who does well, he may find the wife who helped him to reach his elevated position now appears too plain and suburban for his new lifestyle. There is no guarantee that this will lead to divorce, but if there are gaps and changes of direction in the heart line there is a strong indication that the marriage will not stand the changed circumstances.

BRANCH CURVING UPWARDS (Fig. 9.3e)
If there is a small line which branches upwards from the attachment line, the case is similar to the attachment line itself curving upwards, but not so drastic. The partner will be successful, but this should not be particularly stressful to the marriage; this may show a successful

hobby or interest for the partner.

BUBBLE ON ATTACHMENT LINE (Fig. 9.3f)

The partner will be very ill or have some pretty desperate problem to overcome. This kind of mark may appear at the time of trouble and slip away again some time later.

PARALLEL LINES (Fig. 9.3g)

The partners coexist for years but the marriage is not emotionally close or satisfying.

their hands may notice this for themselves and in some cases make the connection with what is going on.

WIDOWHOOD LINE (Fig. 9.5j)

Sometimes this is called the spinster line (this must be clear and unbroken). It is as if these people should never be married at all, because their mates usually die suddenly. Malcolm has seen this line in a woman who has lost three husbands.

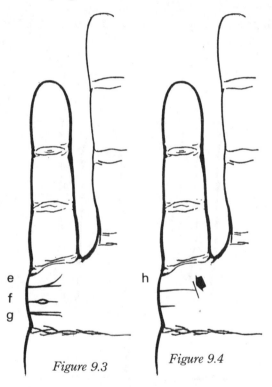

Figure 9.3

Figure 9.4

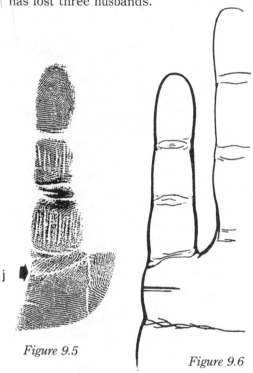

Figure 9.5

Figure 9.6

DELETION LINE (Fig. 9.4h)

We call this a deletion line because it often appears when a marriage is breaking up and the new line vanishes again some time after the divorce, settlement and fuss is over. The new line seems to 'strike out' the attachment line and the marriage just as if a word is being deleted from a piece of text. Clients who are accustomed to looking at

COMPANION LINES (Fig. 9.6)

These exceptionally fine lines which accompany the attachment line indicate that the subject is not completely fulfilled by marriage alone *however close and apparently successful the relationship*. The subject may be deeply committed to an interesting career or a fascinating hobby.

In some cases there will be a need for affairs or other relationships on the side. The reason for this could just possibly be figured out from the way that the heart line curves. If it curves up toward the Jupiter finger, but with the line weakening and softening toward the end, this could imply that the marriage, although good in many ways, leaves the subject sexually unfulfilled. If the heart line starts to curve upwards, then turns and curves sharply downwards toward the head line, there could be a need for close relationships with the subject's own sex. This may be on a companionship basis only, but there could be a degree of latent homosexuality hidden there. This is rather difficult to sort out on the hand; we do advise the reader *not* to remark openly on this to the client as it might be unnecessarily upsetting. It is also worth pointing out that we *all* have masculine and feminine tendencies within us; we would be inhuman if we did not.

If the heart line is straight the subject may find work far more interesting than his companion. He may look down on his partner and consider her needs to be unimportant to him.

Child Lines

These are fine vertical lines which are found near the edge of the hand on the mount of Mercury beneath the Mercury finger and usually crossing the attachment lines (see Fig. 9.7). These lines can be very deceptive and even experienced palmists find them difficult to read. The best way to read them is to hold the skin together between your thumb and forefinger. Roll the skin slightly; try compressing and stretching the skin, looking at it through a magnifying glass. It is difficult to take clear prints of this area of the hand.

If these lines are present, the subject will most probably give life to one or more children and would also look after them personally. Sometimes a subject will actually have children but no corresponding lines or the lines may be so faint that they are easily missed in a poor light with the naked eye. This shows that the subject hardly spends any time in taking care of children *whether he or she has them or not*; indeed there may be no interest in them at all. This is a rare thing to find on a woman's hand but it can happen because the woman has either by choice or circumstance turned her back on her children and concentrated her interests and energies elsewhere.

People who work with children, or look after them for others, have a lot of these fine lines, but on close examination with a magnifying glass, they can be seen to approach, but not touch, the attachment lines.

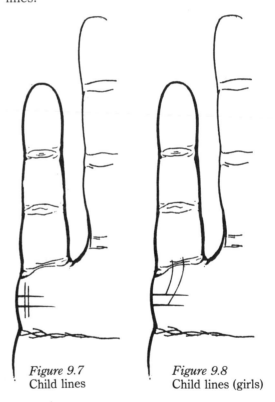

Figure 9.7
Child lines

Figure 9.8
Child lines (girls)

SONS OR DAUGHTERS? (Fig. 9.8)

Some palmists hold the view that vertical lines indicate sons and lines that lean slightly toward the diagonal indicate daughters. This actually seems to work out in many cases but is not a 100 per cent accurate. Another view is that a strong line is a male child and a fine line, a female child. It might be worth making a guess, as there is a fair chance that one would be right.

CHILD LINES THAT TURN AWAY FROM THE ATTACHMENT LINES (Fig. 9.9)

We call a line like this a 'wandering child line'. This ties up with the kind of situation where a child distances itself from its parents. There may be friction between them or it maybe just that the world offers the child more opportunity elsewhere. If in addition the subject's life line hugs the mount of Venus rather closely and the mount of Luna is insignificant, the subject's placid, homely and unadventurous attitude could frustrate the child who would want to branch out and broaden his or her horizons. It is in this way, by educated deduction, that one builds up a picture of the subject's life and character and the surrounding events and circumstances.

BROKEN CHILD LINE (Fig. 9.10)

This indicates a problem with the child. There may be a difficult relationship between the child and the subject or possibly something physically wrong with the child. Either way, it signifies that the relationship is not easy and that the child causes the parent some anguish. An island on a child line shows temporary problems for the child.

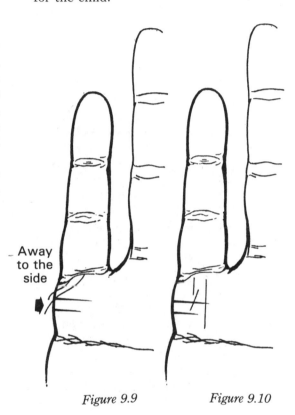

Figure 9.9   *Figure 9.10*

The Girdle of Venus

This line is a kind of supplement to the heart line and it is a sign of emotional sensitivity. Those readers who know a bit about astrology could consider this line Piscean in its nature and far more like the planet Neptune in its influence on the subject than comfortable, materialistic Venus!

It is sometimes present in its entirety on the hand, more often broken pieces of it appear; many people have no trace of it. The girdle is found on elegant or rounded type hands, long fine hands and even rather bony hands; it is least likely to be seen on broad square shaped hands, thick fleshy ones, very A or V shaped (spatulate) hands or extremely long and narrow hands with 'grasping' fingers and curled nails.

THE GOOD NEWS

With luck, the presence of all or part of the girdle gives artistic or creative gifts. It is a good mark to find on the hand of someone employed in one of the 'caring' professions because it shows the ability to understand other people's pain and suffering. The person with the girdle will be easily moved to tears by a sad film or beautiful music. Someone who exhibits an *apparently* hard exterior will be nursing a very soft centre. They long for love and understanding and have a nature which is super sensitive, emotionally refined and delicate.

A writer with this mark can express himself in poetic and romantic terms. An artist or musician lacking this mark would turn out work that may be technically brilliant but somewhat sterile.

THE BAD NEWS

It is true that the girdle of Venus has a very bad press in most palmistry books, with remarks such as hysterical and over-emotional attached to it. This *can* be the case, especially if there is a long whispy-looking head line which dips down toward the mount of Luna. There may be an overreaction to imagined slights and occasional bouts of depression. These subjects would burst into tears on the slightest provocation; they could even become self-destructive when trying to cope with angry feelings; they do not, by and large, try to destroy others. The pent-up nervous energy could be released in overeating, drinking, or at the lowest end of the scale, drug abuse or sexual perversion. These people never forget a slight and are forever wary of anyone who takes advantage of them. Once their trust in a person has gone, it is impossible for them to regain it.

Life is never easy for the possessors of this line. They are idealistic, unrealistic and easily hurt. They can suffer inwardly from disenchantment with a life which does not come up to their unrealistic and over-romantic expectations. This may lead to inner loneliness (especially where there is a straight heart line) and emotional withdrawal.

THE GIRDLE OF VENUS WITH MANY ATTACHMENT LINES

This shows difficulty in staying faithful to one partner, possibly because he or she is continually searching for the perfect mate.

LOVE AND THE GIRDLE

These over-romantic subjects will suffer badly from calf love when young. Then, having learned the hard way just how painful love can be, will go head over heels another couple of times at least just to rub the message in.

FRAGMENTS OF THE GIRDLE (Fig. 9.11)

The area which a complete girdle would encompass can be divided into three sections: A, B and C (see page 113, Fig. 9.12). If only part of the girdle is visible, then refer to the relevant section.

SECTION A OF THE GIRDLE OF VENUS (Fig. 9.12)

This starts under the Jupiter finger or between the Jupiter and Saturn fingers. It curls round under the Saturn finger. Its presence shows the need for emotional security and for respect, career and financial security.

If this section extends into section B the subject will be prepared to disrupt personal life in order to achieve career aims.

If, in addition, the lower part of the life line (situated on the 'southern' part of the hand) also extends outwards toward the fate line this subject is sacrificing his personal life in favour of a career.

FIG. 9.13

If the fate line runs into section A of the girdle, and the life line reaches out toward the fate line, then the subject is definitely career minded and will put his heart and soul into his work.

If the subject has a girdle, plus a life line which curves fairly tightly around the base of the mount of Venus, he will look for emotional fulfilment rather than career fulfilment.

FIG. 9.14

If the subject has section A and section C of the girdle but not section B, he will relate to people on an intellectual level. He might therefore become infatuated with a teacher at school, be taken in by someone with the gift of the gab, or be drawn to someone who understands him on a spiritual level.

SECTION B (Fig. 9.15)

(A) If the A and B sections of the girdle are *both* present, the subject could walk out on a marriage if it interferes with personal aims and ambitions.

(B) This is the most oversensitive and unsettled part of the girdle. When it is present, the subject overreacts to imagined insults, and creates unnecessary problems and complications for himself. The mid-life crisis time of the early forties really unsettles these people, making them restless. They then try to change their lives in some dramatic way. Men, in particular, want to feel that they are still attractive to young women — this can lead to any amount of mayhem.

SECTION C

This section starts between the Apollo and Mercury fingers and curls down under the Apollo finger. We call this the need to be with like-minded people. It appears on the hands of subjects who badly need to communicate. They want to be understood and will seek out people who are on the same spiritual or emotional wavelength. Their interests may be highly intellectual, certainly rather individual, therefore they would choose their friends carefully. They may choose people who can teach them something, as they are impressionable and want to learn. At worst these people find that later in life they have little left in common with their spouse.

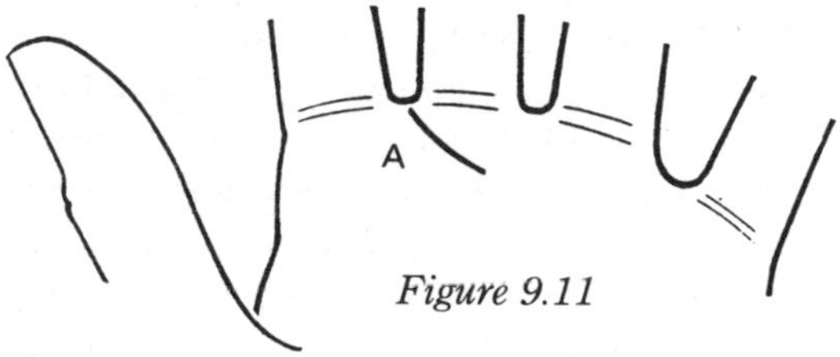

Figure 9.11

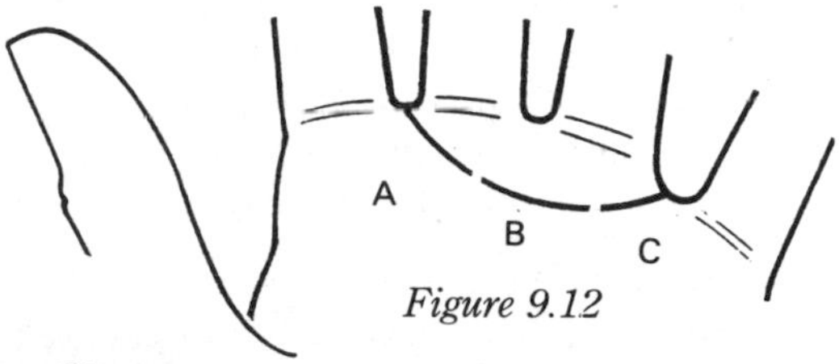

Figure 9.12

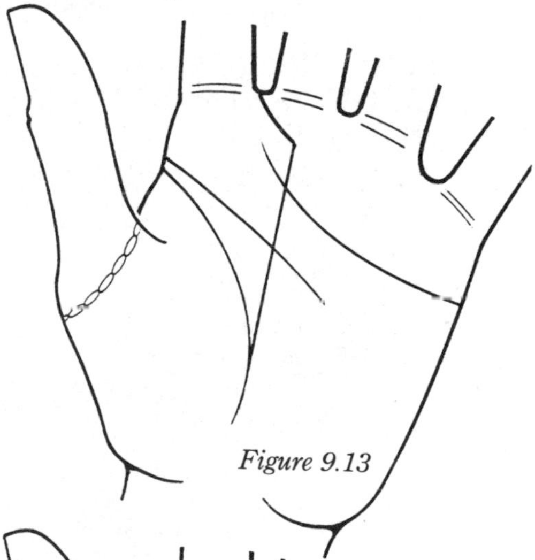

Figure 9.13

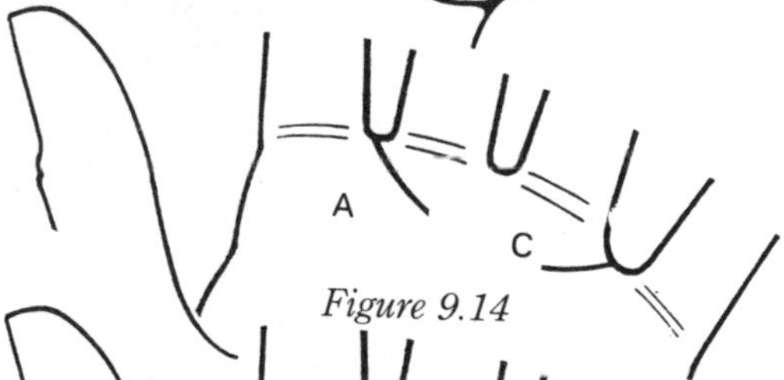

Figure 9.14

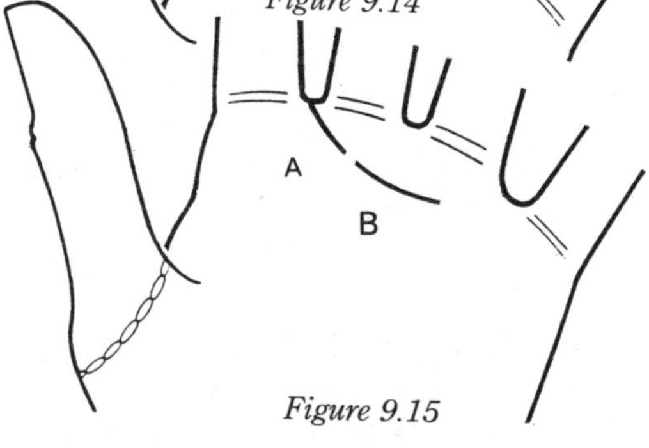

Figure 9.15

GIRDLE OF VENUS WITH A 'TIED' HEAD AND LIFE LINE

This shows the palmist what the subject was like as a child: sensitive, shy, wary of other children and probably afraid of adults — probably with justification.

If the head line curves down to Luna, the childish imagination adds to the situation, creating a fearful phobic child who either felt unsafe when outside the protection of his own home, or worse still, dreadfully unsafe within the home.

Girdles heighten the effects of all traumas. In psychological terms, they show the palmist that this person sitting in front of them is emotionally and physically 'at risk'. The risks vary according to age and circumstances.

Traumas which occur at about the age of twenty to twenty-one can also be spotted on the mount of Neptune. There may be a short life line or an island on the southern end of the life line or fate line. In addition to the girdle, there may on a young person's hand, be a wart on the mount of Luna or Venus — more of this in Chapter 11.

Case Histories

ROBERT: STRONGLY-MARKED GIRDLE OF VENUS ON BOTH HANDS (Fig. 9.16)

The prints from this young man show an unbroken girdle of Venus on the right hand and a very nearly continuous one on the left. We must study not only the girdle but any of the surrounding lines which are

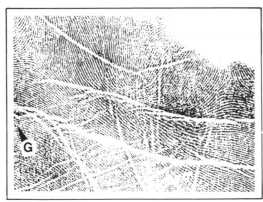

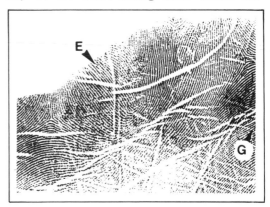

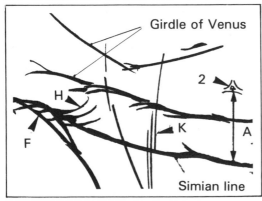

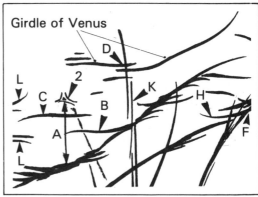

Figure 9.16a Dominant right hand

Figure 9.16b Minor left hand

emotional in content. These exceptionally strong girdles will give him constant problems with his emotions which may cloud his thinking and affect his day-to-day life. He has a whorl on the finger of Apollo which tells us that he tends only to see his own point of view or be rather self-absorbed when dealing with his affections.

Notice the isolated line on the left hand which is near the lines of affection (C). Is this another girdle or a stunted attempt at an extra heart line? If so, this would indicate a lively and animated character (see Chapter 7). To find the answer to this we must look for a datum point[1] on both of the hands. (The datum points are the triradii[2] which appear on both hands.)

Look at the left hand. Take a line (A) down the hand from the triradii, the same length as (A) on the left hand. This will cross the isolated line and land on a strangely thickened part of the heart line. On the right hand, a path drawn down from the triradii ends up on a peculiar addition to the head line which is in fact an embryo simian line! This subject knows deep down what love is, but is so mixed up that he is unable to express it.

WHAT ARE HIS CHANCES?
The strong attachment lines show that he is interested in marriage. He will change in his mid-thirties when the Apollo line changes and crosses the girdle; it actually *breaks* (D) the strangle hold of the girdle in the left hand as it crosses it. There is a strong line which flicks upwards from the heart line reaching up toward the attachment line (B) which shows him reaching out toward a relationship.

He knows how to flirt (the fine lines which fall down from the heart line show

this). Flirting keeps him in touch with the opposite sex and gives him the chance to chat to girls and learn a little more about his feelings.

LET'S PROBE A LITTLE DEEPER
The triradii on the mount of Mercury show his desire to communicate, and the girdle shows his need to be understood, but the heart line of affections makes this difficult, possibly through shyness. Difficult early experiences or even some doubt as to his sexual tendencies or the quality of his performance may haunt him while he is young.

If the area between Mercury and Apollo is high, then he may find it easier to talk to animals (or computers) than humans, but he could make use of the loop of humour on his left hand (E) to cover up awkwardness and embarrassment. The humour loop curls under the finger of Apollo which shows some inner vanity. This, coupled with the whorl on the Apollo finger, would indicate that he could fear a loss of composure during lovemaking or a loss of control over his life if he were to fall deeply in love.

The 'cat's cradle' effect (F) on the tied life and head lines and heavy crossing 'family' lines (G) from the mount of Venus, suggest that he found his teenage years very difficult. He could have hated school or college and bent over backwards to please over-critical parents. The upward 'flick' on the head/life line (H) shows that he could have dreamed about getting out of the situation. He seems to be a dutiful son, never quite shaking off the heavy weight of parentally-imposed guilts.

The change in the Apollo line might indicate the growth of adult confidence due to success in material matters. This would have to be backed up by nice clear successful-looking head and fate lines. The relationship which is due to happen in his thirties (K) indicates that he is definitely interested in marriage but finds it hard to be totally committed. He could become disappointed when he discovers that his

---

[1] *Datum point* A mark which can be used to date a particular event on a particular line — or in this case to determine what a particular line actually is.

[2] *Triradii* (s. triradius) Triangular skin pattern.

woman turns out to be human and not the sugar-plum fairy (see the doubled attachment lines L).

He needs freedom to put his energy into other projects, he may also tend to choose partners who have problems because he is gifted with sympathy and understanding. The partner's problems and responsibilities sometimes show up as companion lines (K) to the attachment lines (L). This subject is prepared to 'look after' another but may keep his real needs well hidden for fear of rejection. This hand shows a personality which is using a variety of survival mechanisms in order to get through life. Good experiences will help to offset his super sensitivity whereas unfortunate ones will reinforce his poor self-image thereby increasing the risk of unhappy relationships.

PETER: GIRDLE OF VENUS ON THE MINOR LEFT HAND (Fig. 9.17)

The 'southern' area of the hand, that is the *heel* of the hand, can throw light on early experiences which shape our attitudes. The area comprises the mount of Venus on the radial (thumb) side of the hand, the mount of Luna on the ulna (percussion) side and the mount of Neptune in the middle (see Fig. 1.1).

In this example we have a man who is still living at home at a time when he should be out on his own, because he is caught between his own oversensitive nature, and the demands of his parents who do not want to relinquish their influence over him. He has a weak-looking life line, showing a low level of physical energy, little zest for life and a lack of self-confidence. He gives way for the sake of peace.

The line of Mars (or companion line to the life line) shows that he *could* draw on extra strength under severe pressure. He has a long sloping head line which shows a very active imagination, and a wart on the mount of Luna which points to a

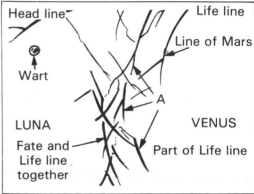

Figure 9.17 Minor left hand

(temporary) state of nervous fearfulness. The broken bits of life line (marked A) show that he wants to become independent and to have a home and family of his own, but the inner confusion, coupled with his overprotective parents, make it hard for him to go out and find himself a mate. If he screwed up his courage and broke out of his paralysis, the lines would start to grow a little clearer and the wart would drop off! All of which goes to show that we can change our 'fate' if we want to.

COMBINATION OF A TRAUMATIC EVENT AND A SENSITIVE NATURE: KEVIN — GIRDLE OF VENUS ON THE DOMINANT RIGHT HAND (Fig. 9.18)

This print was taken from a young man about five years *before* he was involved in a tragic accident. There is an obstruction line

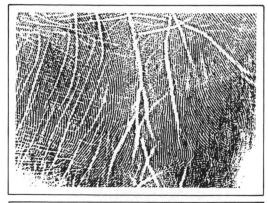

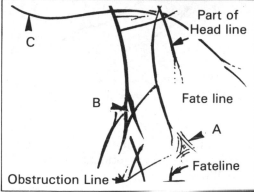

Figure 9.18 Dominant right hand coming from the chained family line (C). The obstruction line crosses a busy junction of the fate and head lines which meets another stray obstruction line reaching out from the life line.

The accident occurred when Kevin and his friend were out on their motor cycles travelling down a country road. His friend's bike went out of control, hit an embankment and slewed across the road in front of him, giving him no time to manoeuvre his bike out of the way. He drove straight into his friend and killed him outright; there was no way that he could have avoided hitting him.

The junction of lines which cross the steeply sloping head line shows the disturbing effect on his mind, and the triradii (A) which appear in the gap in the fate line, plus the island (B) on the life line show that he will have to find a way of coming to terms with the accident or else it will spoil his mental equilibrium for the rest of his life. There seems to be another lesser trauma at the age of twenty-four; perhaps this may give him an opportunity to bring this event out into the open and then put it away into the past perspective for good and all.

Sibling Lines

This is a new concept which we are throwing out to other hand readers for research and consideration. We have been looking at these for a couple of years now, and the theory does seem to fit the facts.

WHERE ARE THEY AND WHAT ARE THEY? (Fig. 9.19)

Sibling lines are located on the edge of the hand on the *radial* side of the mount of Jupiter. They look rather like the attachment lines and their meaning is somewhat similar, but the relationships that they are concerned with are those of *siblings* or, in plain English, brothers and sisters.

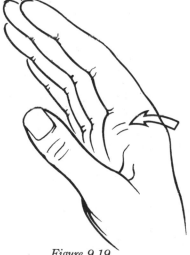

Figure 9.19

Malcolm has always associated these lines with people who can adapt to a variety of jobs. Our two ideas might be connected because someone who grew up in a rough and tumble environment will be more adaptable in life than someone who learned to live as a single child among adults.

NUMBER OF LINES
It would be nice to say 'one line equals one sibling, two equal two', but it does not work quite that way. A person's *feelings* about those he considers close to him are more important in this area. Someone who grew up in a close relationship with a neighbourhood friend would carry the same kind of line. Someone who hated all but one of his siblings might only have one strongly-marked line.

NO SIBLING LINES
When there are no real lines in this area, or only small shapeless skin formations, it would be safe to say that the subject grew up in a household where there were no other young people, and/or did not relate easily to other children. The self-sufficiency, even aloofness, that this environment produces would make for an independent attitude and a poor team member late in life. Look also for whorls on the thumbs and fingertips.

ONE STRONG LINE
If the area is clear but for one strong line, the person is attached to one sibling. The chances are that the subject has one sister, brother or very close childhood friend. It is possible that there *were* others around but there is only one strong attachment.

TWO STRONG LINES
Similar to the one line: an attachment or a feeling of attachment to two siblings.

TWO OR THREE LINES BUT ONLY ONE STANDING OUT STRONGLY
This person grew up among a large family

or in a household where there were other young people around. The one strong line shows a lasting attachment to one of them.

POOR RELATIONS (Fig. 9.20a)

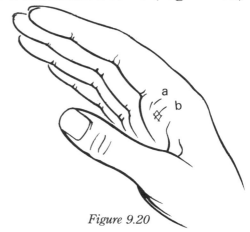

Figure 9.20

If a person has poor relationships with his siblings, he tends to move away from them geographically and emotionally later in life. He will have as little as possible to do with them, therefore the lines gradually fade away. If there is an on and off relationship — better still, one that is broken and then mended again — the sibling line will show a break and a fresh start (a).

PROBLEMS
If the subject is aware that his sibling(s) have a problem, there will be an echo of this on his own hand. Here are some of the substantiated problems which we have seen.

SQUARE OVER SIBLING LINE (Fig. 9.20b)
A square is a sign of protection/frustration; therefore this would suggest one of the subject's siblings is hemmed in by problems and that the subject, of course, is aware of this.

CROSS, ISLAND, STAR, ANY OTHER DISTORTING MARKS (Fig. 9.21)
A cross, star, or messy area at the tail end

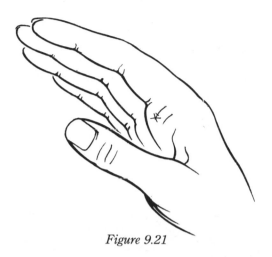

Figure 9.21

of a line shows severe problems. The subject would be aware of his sibling's unhappiness and could try to help the sufferer out of trouble. A client with a star here told us that her sister had been injured in a car accident, became an alcoholic and died very young. The doctors said that she had suffered severe brain damage in the accident.

An island on a sibling line can show the presence of a sibling who is mentally or physically handicapped.

REDNESS

Redness around one of these lines indicates great awareness of the sibling's problems at the time of the reading. If there is a star, cross, breaks or other distorting marks, there could either be some sort of quarrel going on between the parties, but it is much more likely that the subject wants to give help.

SASHA'S TALE

I become aware of these lines whilst giving a reading a few years ago. The lady whose hand I was reading had a great deal of redness plus a starry formation on and around one of these lines and on impulse I asked her if she had a sister or brother who was having problems. She told me that her sister had just given birth to a first child and that it was a Down's Syndrome baby. She told me that her sister was utterly pole-axed by this, and that although the sister's husband was a very kind and supportive man, he also seemed temporarily unable to cope. My client said that she would help in any way she could, and would probably become very involved in the upbringing of the child which would enable her sister to go ahead and have other children if she wanted to.

My client, herself a mature lady at the time, had never married and was successfully running her own business from home. She was in a position to give this child love and her sister and brother-in-law the help they needed, so in a way it seemed as if this baby was destined to bring love and fulfilment to a family rather than the bitterness and disappointment that might have been the case.

CHAPTER TEN

The Minor Lines

Via lasciva (Fig. 10.1)

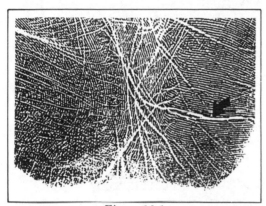

Figure 10.1

This used to be called the poison or allergy line. Both are correct as an allergy shows that 'one man's meat is another man's poison'. It is found on the mount of Luna travelling toward Venus. The shape and size varies from one hand to another, as does the meaning.

If the line stands out long and clear, the body and mind are sensitive to drugs, chemicals and certain foods. These people need only a small amount of any drug for the body to react; therefore they tend to turn naturally to homoeopathy and natural remedies because the body dislikes synthetic substances so much. This line shows healing and self-healing abilities. Allergies are indicated when the line wraps around the percussion side of Luna, even if there is *no* via lasciva as such; but if there are two or three strong lines on the percussion side of Luna, allergies and allergic ailments like migraine will be present. If these lines have v formations at the side, there is even more evidence.

If the via lasciva is broken, islanded or surrounded by fine lines, there may be a craving for outside stimulants such as drugs and drink.

Food cravings, especially chocolate, are amazingly common with this line. Chocolate is known to have a tranquillizing effect. It is also worth noting that this area of the hand is where we find evidence of diabetes.

If the subject has small hands with even slightly pointy fingers, there could be a real weight problem due to his (or more likely her) rushing to the fridge or the sweetie cupboard every time life gets trying.

If the line reaches the life line its effect will be more profound and obvious in daily life. There may even be slight brain damage due to overadministration of anaesthetic at some stage! It is a good idea to look for islands, a 'string of pearls' effect and damage to the head line for corroboration.

The via lasciva is confusing to interpret

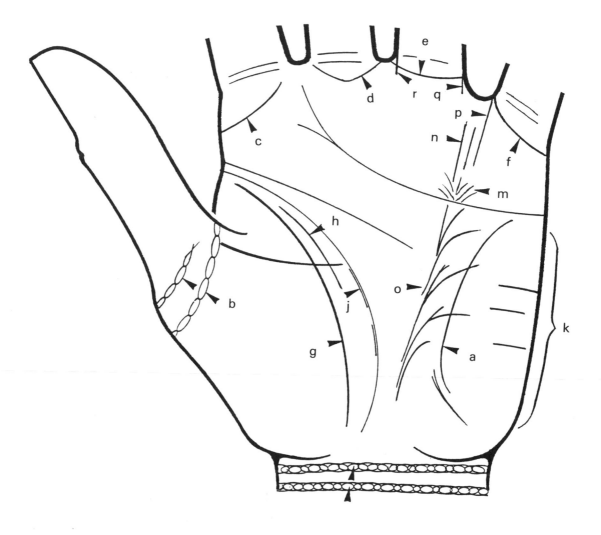

Figure 10.2 Minor lines

because it is on the area of the hand associated with travel. If it stands clean and
clear on a hand with only an average-sized
mount of Luna and a life line that curls
round the mount of Venus, the subject will
not be especially interested in travel. If it is
deep and seems to pull at the lower end of
the life line, tugging it away from Venus,
there could be at least one important
journey overseas, probably in connection
with family and friends who live abroad.
(For other information on travel, see page
126).

CURVE OF INTUITION (Fig. 10.2a)

This shows intuition and probably psychic
gifts. For confirmation of this look for a
ring of Solomon, high mount of Neptune,
healing marks, girdle of Venus, spiritual
marks.

FAMILY RING (Fig. 10.2b)

This shows the home base. If there are two
rings the subject could be involved with
two families, two homes, dots and discolor-
ation show problems at that time. Lines

radiating from the line indicate family interference in the subject's life if they cut across the life line. A strong line like a light crease is frequently seen radiating out from the family line. If it reaches out and touches the life line, the subject feels a sense of loyalty to his family. If the crease turns northwards, the parents are much loved; if southwards the love is directed towards the children, or to a later marriage partner.

RING OF SOLOMON OR 'CARING' LINE (Fig. 10.2c)

A friend of ours called Sheila McGuirk, who is an excellent palmist, donated the following bit of information. This belongs to people who help others. If the heart line leads into this the subject will only be happy working in a caring job, indeed looking after others may take the place of normal family life.

RING OF SATURN (Fig. 10.2d)

This is an unfortunate sign as it suppresses the personality and cuts off the balancing influence of the Saturn finger from the rest of the hand. This belongs to a lone wolf who finds it difficult to relate to others and join in with social activities.

RING OF APOLLO (Fig. 10.2e)

There is no specific meaning to this mark except that it is some kind of blocking mechanism.

SPINSTER LINE (Fig. 10.2f)

This is sometimes called the ring of Mercury. This *must* curve away from the crease line where the finger joins the hand and it must be unbroken. It belongs to people who either do not marry or who repeatedly lose partners, usually through death. It is the 'I've buried three husbands' syndrome. (See Fig. 9.5.)

LINE OF MARS (Fig. 10.3 and Fig. 10.2g)

This is sometimes called the sister line or

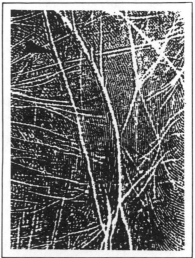

Father

Daughter

Figure 10.3

inner life line because it sits on the inside of the life line. It is a strong line, often as deeply engraved as the life line itself. There are several interpretations for this, the usual one being that it provides strength and protection to the part of the life line that it follows; this is especially so if the life line is chained, broken or islanded. We have found that people with this line are given inner strength and vitality to overcome illness or accidents. They seem to be less open to viruses than others. If this line travels for the length of the life line, as the print shows, the protection will last throughout life.

The line can enter the hand at any age and stay to help during particular periods in one's life. The Mars line is also considered to be one's inner spiritual pathway, giving protection and awareness of the spiritual self. The line may come and go in the hand as the spiritual interplay goes on.

The line of Mars is found on the hands of healers and others with an inner calling. The prints (Fig. 10.3) which we have shown are of a father and daughter. The father is a medium and healer, the daughter is too young to have discovered any particular spiritual pathway yet. The father says that he has always felt inwardly guided through-out his life. He also pointed out to us that he has the Sun and Moon in the mystical sign of Pisces.

MEDIAL LINE (Fig. 10.2h)

This lies between the line of Mars and the life line and indicates that there was some sort of an early start that was quickly recognized as being wrong. The subject may have married in order to please the parents, gone to university or gone into a career designed to live out the parents' dreams. Either way there is an early realization that it has not worked out. The difference between this and the line of Mars is that the person is more likely to put up with the problem and live through it rather than take his or her courage (Mars equals courage) in both hands and make the break.

SHADOW LINES (Fig. 10.2j)

You will sometimes see a fine tracery of two or three lines accompanying the life line round Venus. These are said to show friendships, but they also seem to show spirit guides or dead members of the subject's family still keeping a fond and helpful eye on him.

TRAVEL LINES (Fig. 10.2k)

These are on the percussion and may or may not include the via lasciva among them. They can appear at any point from the heart line down to the wrist. Many faint marks around the percussion are a sign of restlessness but not necessarily of real journeys. One or two deep lines will show very few journeys but they could be very distant and certainly memorable. If one or two of the lines join up with the fate, Apollo or any other northward travelling line, many of the journeys will have a purpose; this could be in connection with business etc. Other indications of travel are a life line which reaches outwards toward Luna, a high mount of Luna, a mount of Pluto (lower Luna) which reaches down toward the rascettes, callouses on the hands from carrying suitcases plus a well-filled photo album! See page 126 for more detailed information on travel lines.

HEALTH LINE (Fig. 10.2o)

This is a very confusing line. It appears on the hands of the healthy as well as the sick and is often seen on the hands of healers, nurses and other people who look after the sick. It shows up strongly on the hands of people who look after sick relatives or bring up delicate children. The **healing lines** (Fig. 10.2n) are an extension of the health line. Time and time again we have noticed that people who quite unwittingly have healing abilities are drawn to those who need help. It is as if there were a hidden force giving these people a spiritual push. Other people's health seems to be important to these people. If you take a look at the hands of a healer after he has used his gifts, you will see a reddish patch under the health line; this will fade away after an hour or so.

If the line is broken up and flakes upwards and outwards toward the ulna side as illustrated, there could be heavy responsibilities on behalf of sick relatives; also look for family aggravation lines radiating out from Venus. This formation is also found on the hands of people who try to control their children by 'give, give, giving' to them, a form of keeping them dependent.

Minor Lines

HEALING OR MEDICAL STRIATA (Fig. 10.2n)

There can be two, three or more lines but always set in the position as illustrated. Sometimes these lines are crossed by a diagonal line. Not only doctors and nurses have this, but also spiritual healers, counsellors, psychiatrists, hypnotherapists and any other person who helps in a specialized way. These people are very good at helping their family and friends when they become sick and do so without complaining. They appear to be spiritually directed toward helping and caring.

HELPING LINES (Fig. 10.2m)

These are lots of fine lines rising from the heart line as illustrated, and belong to people who work with the general public in shops, hospitals etc.

LINE LEADING TO THE INSIDE OF THE MERCURY FINGER (Fig. 10.2p)

This shows teaching abilities. The teaching will be more formal if there is another line converging; more spiritual and mediumistic if the line is connected to the medical striata.

FINE LINES BETWEEN MERCURY AND APOLLO (Fig. 10.2q)

This shows spiritual growth, consciousness gained by the spiritual self on this earth. If we close our fingers tightly, the amount of daylight we can see at the base of the fingers shows our subconscious mind is open to the unknown forces around us. The lines from the inside of the fingers reaching down to the mounts show how consciously we live by this awareness and how we help others with what gifts we may have.

These lines may connect with the c section of the girdle of Venus (see Chapter 9), which shows a need to be with people who have the same interests.

FINE LINES ON THE INSIDE OF APOLLO ON THE SATURN SIDE (Fig. 10.2r)

Two parallel lines show that the person will never be alone in life. If these lines converge, the subject will never be without a physical and emotional relationship. These connection lines appear at the end of one's lifespan, therefore they may line one up to meet people in the next existence. Could they even be a foreshadowing of one's next incarnation?

LINES BETWEEN JUPITER AND SATURN

See heart line (Chapter 7) for this section.

TRIDENT ON THE MOUNT OF APOLLO

Three little lines like the forks of a trident at the top of the Apollo mount show that the subject will always find money from somewhere. Even when the debts begin to pile up, these people will be able to earn or gain the money they need, often in the nick of time. A blank area at the top of Apollo means financial losses or home and security are no longer satisfactory.

COUNTRIES VISITED (Fig. 10.4)

It may sound crazy but it is possible to show where a person goes on his travels. There is no logic to this, it just works. Just see where the lines are and check with your subject for confirmation. (We have recently had this confirmed by our friend, palmist, Ashwin Pandya.)

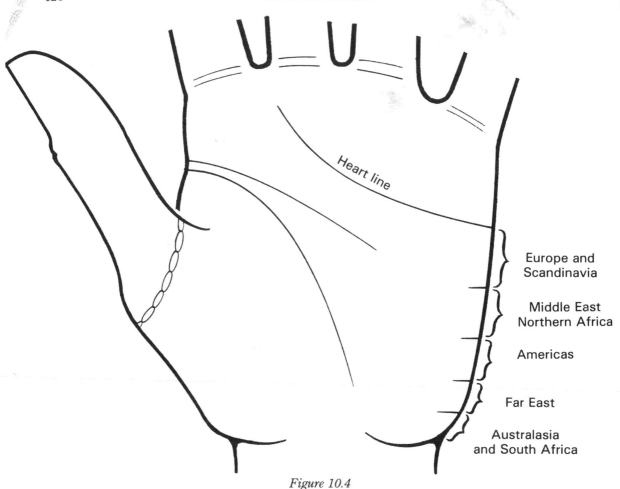

Figure 10.4

Place the percussion side of your own hand onto the picture lining up your heart line with the heart line in the picture. Then look at the countries you are likely to visit.

(a)   Between the heart and head line: Scandinavia and Europe.

(b)   Around the end of the head line: the Middle East. Oddly enough, important business dealings *which do not always involve actual travel* are also seen as lines at this point.

(c)   Long strong lines on the Mars/Luna junction: the USA and Canada; also possible but less likely are the Caribbean and South America.

(d)   Mid Luna: India, Sri Lanka, Seychelles.

(e)   Lower Luna: China, Korea, Japan.

(f)   Pluto: Australia, New Zealand.

TRAVEL LINES WHICH TUG AT THE LIFE LINE (Fig. 10.5)

Sometimes a travel line touches a branch which shoots out from the life line. This indicates some long-term involvement with a foreign country. A typical example would be of a parent whose child has gone to live permanently abroad. This obviously creates an interest in the politics and economics of that country which would not have arisen otherwise. Of course there would be visits to the country in question and possibly a genuine link developing with its people and culture. I have seen this kind

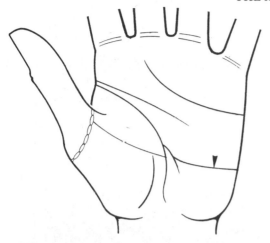

Figure 10.5 This kind of formation would be found on the hands of someone who had links with Canada or the USA.

of thing happen to my Jewish friends whose children have settled and married in Israel.

This kind of link with a foreign country can occur as a result of friendships made on holiday with people of a different nationality.

EXAMPLE 1: SARAH, AN ARTIST (Fig. 10.6)

Sarah was born in the USA and came to England at the age of twenty-three and has stayed ever since. The line coming from the point where the family line touches the life line shows how another country 'tugged' at her life line.

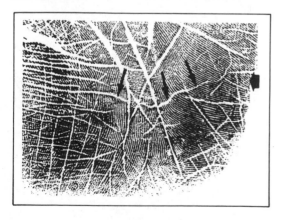

Figure 10.6

EXAMPLE 2: JENNIFER (Fig. 10.7)

Jennifer is now twenty-two and is working in England for the time being. She knows that when her work permit runs out she will have to return to Pakistan. Apart from the travel line touching the life line there is a hint of her apprehension in the line from Venus which is just under the skin.

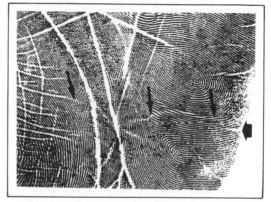

Figure 10.7

EXAMPLE 3: LAWRENCE (Fig. 10.8)

Lawrence is seven years old and was born in Switzerland. His family went to live in Argentina. It is interesting to note that in his mother's hand there is a line running from the family line to the correct position for Argentina. (See the lower arrow on Lawrence's hand for position of Argentina.)

Figure 10.8

RITA: CHANGES OF COUNTRY SHOWN ON THE LIFE LINE (Fig. 10.9)

This broken-up life line looks as if it belongs to a person whose life is filled with terrible traumas. It does not; it belongs to someone who has already made her home in a country other than her own and seems to be about to do the same thing again. However, she does seem to have her share of dramas in life but no more than many other people.

Rita was born to a lower middle-class family in Ireland forty years ago. She left there and came to London to train as a nurse (a). She married an Englishman and began to make her home in London. The marriage did not last very long; Rita got a divorce and married another Englishman some time later. This marriage was not too successful either but it was fairly bearable. Rita decided to stick with the marrige this time because by now she had a couple of children. Now she and her husband are about to move to Hong Kong for an un-specified number of years because her husband's job is going to take the pair of them out there (b).

Rita is looking forward to her new life in Hong Kong, but feels that she will come back to London eventually. She still keeps in touch with the remnants of her family in Ireland (c) but feels less and less 'Irish' as her life goes on. She says that she can see herself losing all the links with her birthplace as the years progress.

This print and case history are only concerned with Rita's countries of resi-dence; for health, other events and character implications please refer to the appropriate chapters. Just take a look at the exceptionally strong pieces of life line which jump further and further away from the main line which marks the place of her birth. The faint line of Mars (c) shows that there is still some tie of blood or sentiment to the land of her birth.

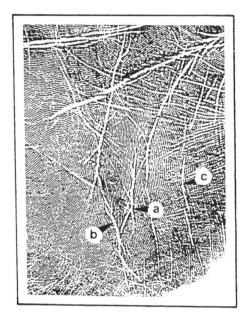

Figure 10.9

MILITARY STIGMATA (Fig. 10.10)

These marks are traditionally supposed to belong to people who spend their lives in the armed services. It does seem to be true, but it also applies to those who, although not in the forces themselves, come from military families. They would also show up on someone who has a long-term involve-ment with something like the scouts or territorials. This also applies to a 'service' wife.

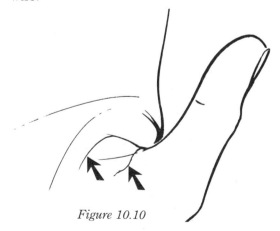

Figure 10.10

CHAPTER ELEVEN

Mark; Modification of Lines; Warts

Marks

The meaning of each mark varies according to the line or mount on which it appears. Each mark should be clear and, if possible, backed up by supporting evidence elsewhere on the hand. Marks are often *temporary* features which appear before an event and fade away some time after.

CROSSES ON LINES (Fig. 11.1 and 11.2)

On the life line: shock, operation, illness. Check the finger nails for horizontal ridges which would confirm shock to the system within the previous few months.

On the fate line: could be almost anything, e.g. money troubles, career setback, emotional upheaval.

There is an area around the lower end of the Apollo line and health line which shows property negotiations. A couple of crosses here mean that several properties are involved. Many crosses show an involvement with a large building such as a school, hospital or hotel.

CROSSES ON MOUNTS

On the mount of Apollo: a faint cross here indicates a win, bonus, a nice surprise. They may be a lucky business deal or money which was not hard to earn. This

Figure 11.1

Figure 11.2

mark is often rather low on the mount, just above the heart line.

On the mount of Jupiter: an interest in teaching. If high on the mount, near the heart line, tradition says marriage to a rich partner, or one who becomes rich.

On the mount of Mercury: coping with a computer or other extremely modern machinery — especially machinery concerned with the storage and retrieval of *information* and for *communication*.

The so-called mystic cross is supposed to

be between the heart and head lines. It is usually made from bits of the fate line and an influence line. Neither of us thinks this is a reliable indication of psychic powers.

Crosses on the side of the first phalange of the Saturn finger seem to show living near large animals, especially horses. Possibly a child line going into the crease line on the Mercury finger may indicate a child working with animals.

Sheila McGuirk tells us that a cross on Luna means that the subject is prone to sea-sickness, possibly to other forms of travel sickness too. She discovered this because she herself is not a good sailor and has checked this with other queasy travellers. We have not checked this ourselves though.

SQUARES (Fig. 11.3)

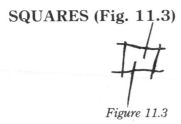

Figure 11.3

A square is like a fence round a building; it protects it but it also restricts free passage. Therefore, a square could indicate a miraculous, possibly spirit-aided escape from danger, or on the other hand sadness and frustration.

SQUARES ON LINES
On the life line: a deeply-etched square enclosing a break shows recovery and protection from physical danger and illness.

On the head line: a deeply-etched square enclosing a break protects from injury to the head or upper body. An elderly client of ours who had this mark confirmed its traditional meaning. She explained that in her youth she had fallen from a horse while hunting and narrowly missed having her head stamped on by one of the following horses.

On any other line: if deeply etched, it seems to be a sign of protection; if very fine

and transitory a sign of frustration, e.g. a light square on the head line tells that the subject is fed up with his job; if on the heart line, emotional restriction, frustration and sadness. If you see this on a client's hand, remember that this is not permanent; light covering marks come and go fairly easily and if the person makes an effort to change the situation the mark will fade.

EXAMPLE OF A SQUARE: CASE HISTORY, PAT (Fig. 11.4)

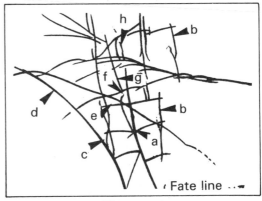

Figure 11.4

The print shows a split on the fate line (a) covered by a square (b) at the point of time when Pat lived through an exceptionally difficult period. Her husband had left her with no money and four small children, one of whom was mentally handicapped. She used her considerable personal courage and reserves as shown by the effort line (c) rising from the life line (d), plus the decision lines (e) which forced her to accept change (f). Pat found herself a job in the accounts section of a local firm (g) which gave her the money to cope, plus self-respect and job satisfaction which compensated for the hardship of her personal life. She also made some good women friends at that time which gave her practical and moral support when she needed it most (h).

SQUARES ON MOUNTS

If you see one of these during a reading, use the guideline of protection/restriction. The exception to this rule would be a square on Jupiter which is both a protection against loss in business and a strong indication of *teaching ability*.

TRIANGLES AND DIAMONDS (Fig. 11.5)

Figure 11.5

A line which splits into an island shaped like a triangle or a diamond indicates a really nasty problem. On the head line this shows intense frustration and feelings of confinement. This could result from a long spell in hospital or even prison; there may just be exceptionally frustrating and confining circumstances at the time shown by the triangular or diamond-shaped island.

Isolated triangles on mounts are a sign of exceptional talent, even brilliance. The particular field will vary according to the mount. A large triangle between the head and heart lines is traditionally supposed, like the mystic cross, to signify strong psychic powers. We have no evidence of this.

STARS (Fig. 11.6)

Figure 11.6

A star is traditionally a malevolent sign. it intensifies energies at its location and acts like a stone piercing and cracking a pane of glass. It could indicate a shock or an accident. A star on Apollo is traditionally supposed to indicate fame and fortune. (Malcolm and Sasha are scanning their hands daily for this sign, but so far no luck.)

GRILLES (Fig. 11.7)

Figure 11.7

Lines are channels of energy, therefore densely-packed lines mean a super-abundance of energy at that point, even hyperactivity. Vertical lines mean excessive wants; horizontal lines, cross purposes or confusion. Therefore, a grille points to obsessive behaviour which takes its nature from the mount it appears on, e.g. on Venus, obsessive desire for something or someone; on Jupiter, obsessive need to be boss.

LINES ON THE LOWER MARS AND THE MOUNT OF VENUS

Small vertical lines and/or grille formations around this area show an ability to keep secrets. A clean area shows that the subject has no interest in secrecy for himself and (possibly) does not see why other people want to be secretive.

TASSELS (Fig. 11.8)

Figure 11.8

Two or more lines flaking away from the main line and running close to each other indicate a loss of energy from that line. In our example on the head line, there may be a lack of calcium fluoride or potassium or just a great deal of worry. This may signify depression or even senile dementia. Tassels on the heart line are completely different.

DOTS (Fig. 11.9)

Figure 11.9

Dots are always important. They show illness and stress at the time of the reading. They are miniature craters which suck energy downwards away from the line or mount on which they appear. The body may be using more energy than it is producing and the subject will soon outrun his natural reserves. Dots of stress can be vitally important if seen on the health area of the heart line. A dot on the head line shows anxiety, other dots have to be read according to the line they are on.

ENLARGED DOTS (Fig. 11.9)

Use a magnifying glass for these small marks. When a dot or crater has a ring around it, this shows that the original cause of the illness or upset is leaving the subject. A good example of this can be seen on the health area of the heart lines of people who are getting over heart troubles.

CHAINS (Fig. 11.10)

Figure 11.10

A subject with chained lines would lack stamina, assertiveness and confidence. He (or more likely she) may have weak health or just a rather lifeless and ineffective character.

If only part of a line is chained, the person will go through a difficult confusing time or a period of weak health. The line which is affected and the placement of the chaining will indicate the nature and the date of the difficulty. There are some specific ailments associated with patches of chaining; these are explained in Chapter 12.

ISLANDS (Fig. 11.11)

Figure 11.11

These are vitally important and must be taken into account on any reading. An island is a problem; it could be health, troubles in relationships, money worries, work problems or any one of a hundred things. The important thing to remember is that an island is an event which is difficult to live through because it suddenly splits the energies of the line it appears upon.

Always check whether an island is an isolated configuration, which is more likely to be a health matter, or if the island has corresponding disturbances on other lines, which would lead one to suspect the onset of a sudden and life-changing event.

OTHER SIGNS

Blotchy or discoloured patches, areas which appear shiny, faded or peculiar in some way usually indicate a health problem. Areas which look red can show anger or tension according to the line or mount.

BRANCHES ON LINES (Fig. 11.12)

Figure 11.12

Branches which rise up from lines show improvements in situations; falling branches show losses and setbacks. On the heart line, falling lines are traditionally supposed to be losses in love, but we have found short ones to be a sign of flirtatiousness.

Special Lines and Marks in the Hands

ISLANDS, NOT CONNECTED WITH ILLNESS (Fig. 11.13)

(a) A large island at the beginning of the life line is unhappiness in childhood.

(b) A thin island on the early part of the life line shows shock or upset. This is frequently the result of getting married and therefore facing up to adult reality!

(c) A long island or thin line close to the life line on the Venus side means a period of restriction. This could be due to looking after parents or children or studying; the restriction is self-imposed to some degree.

(d) An island on the fate line shows a period of worry. This could be due to marriage problems or problems with children, financial difficulties or problems at work.

(e) An island on a line which leads into the fate line means relationship difficulties.

INFLUENCE LINES

(f) Fine lines running parallel to the life

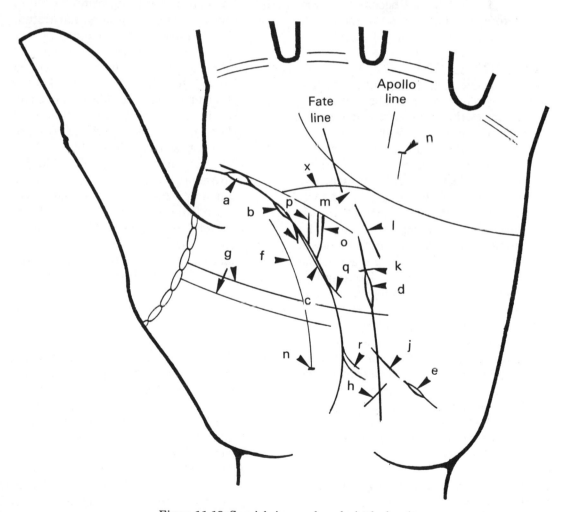

Figure 11.13 Special signs and marks in the hand

line on Venus show relationships or friendships — people who mean a lot to the subject. They may sometimes show an attachment to relatives or friends who are no longer living, but who keep a friendly eye on the subject from the 'other side'. (See Fig. 8.4.)

(g)   Lines radiating out from Venus and crossing other (vertical) lines are interference lines. If they cut through the life line, the interference is overt; if they cut the fate line, the subject will be forced to take some sort of action. If the lines peter out before reaching the life line, the problem is either hidden or becomes solved before coming out into the open; hence their usual title of 'worry' lines.

DECISION LINES

(h)   A fine line at an angle cutting the fate or Apollo lines from the radial side indicates that the subject will take the initiative over a decision.

(j)   A fine line at an angle cutting the fate or Apollo lines from the ulna side indicates a decision made by someone else, possibly the spouse or partner, which will affect the subject. It may also indicate pressure being put on the subject causing decisions to be taken.

(k)   A fine line cutting straight across the fate or Apollo lines is a blocking line which forces the subject to take action. This line can be very short or may be traced back to Venus.

(x)   A line joining the heart and head lines indicates a lack of communication in relationships. The marriage may even come to an end without the two parties talking things over. One or both partners finds it hard to discuss deep feelings. **NB This line must cut the fate line**.

BREAKS IN THE FATE LINE (Fig. 11.13)

A break in the fate line is a change of course, direction or job.

(l)   If the lines overlap, the change will go smoothly; if the new line jumps toward the ulna side it could be a setback or backward step, i.e. less money or not such a good job. If the fate line later alters direction toward Jupiter, the change will work out for the best.

(m)   A break in the fate line with a gap between the two lines means a period of time out of work or a temporarily backward step in life.

(n)   A small blocking line or dot at the end of a line may mean the death of someone close.

(o)   Two lines, one going from the life to the head line in the area illustrated, show restriction by parents. There may be a religious or arranged marriage. See also (c) in this section because both these marks are likely to show up in this case. The parents may be old-fashioned in their outlook or there may just be underlying pressure to marry someone 'suitable'.

(p)   Lines rising from the life line are effort lines. They show the times when the subject is trying to get over a bad patch or is setting out to achieve something for himself. If there is a dot at the base of the effort line, the subject may be getting over an operation.

(q)   Small downward lines on the palmar side of the life line could mean a change of home or job. Take a look at signs on the fate and Apollo lines to back this up.

(r)   As above but longer lines would indicate a restless period, a need for change or excitement in life. This is apparent when parents try to interfere in the subject's life, especially if it cuts the fate line.

(s)   Small downward lines from the life line on the Venus side *may* indicate the number of children but also losses of loved ones, such as grandparents. These light lines are evidence of people entering and leaving the subject's life.

Loops

Loop formation in the skin ridges on the palm are common. Whorls are less common; they have the same meaning as the loops but are more intense.

THE 'RAJAH' LOOP (Fig. 11.14a)

This rarely-seen loop, which has an additional triradius, reaches down between the Jupiter and Saturn fingers. It is supposed to bring power and status. People who have this loop are usually good looking and often arrogant.

THE LOOP OF SERIOUS INTENT (Fig. 11.14b)

Between the Saturn and Apollo fingers, this commonly seen loop indicates a serious turn of mind, someone who makes an effort to read, learn and understand.

LOOP OF HUMOUR (Fig. 11.14c)

Between Mercury and Apollo, this loop shows a sense of humour, also a love or words, writing, communicating etc. If this area is high, there will be a love of animals; but if the area is high and crisscrossed by marks, the subject loves animals but has little time to devote to them. If the centre of this loop forms a whorl, the subject will have a talent for foreign languages.

LOOP OF MEMORY (Fig. 11.14e)

This loop is found near the end of the head line. It gives a good memory and also the ability to use contacts from one's past to help one in business etc. This person keeps in touch with people on a purely social level as well.

LOOP OF IMAGINATION (Fig. 11.14f)

This loop gives imagination and intuition which seems more likely to be used purposefully if near the Mars mount. A whorl shows psychic gifts. Loops in this Luna area also show a love of the countryside and of associated sports such as fishing.

VANITY LOOP OR LOOP OF STYLE (Fig. 11.14d)

Between Mercury and Apollo, reaching round beneath the Apollo finger, this loop is supposed to be a sign of vanity. We have found that people with this mark take pride in themselves and what they do, or have great personal style. They can be very sarcastic and cutting when cross.

Warts

We know that warts can be charmed away, maybe helped away, as one never knows when they are due to come or go and by the time one finds a wart charmer they may be on their way out anyway! According to the medical profession, warts are caused by a virus but seen in palmistry terms their cause is psychosomatic. They indicate long-term stress situations requiring changes that only we ourselves can bring about, problems that only we ourselves can overcome.

The placing of the wart gives a clue to its meaning. If found on the Jupiter mount or finger there would be something standing in the way of one's progress out in the world. There could be a knock to the subject's ambition and pride, a lack of confidence and self-identity.

Warts are most frequently found on the Saturn mount. If there is one here or on the Saturn finger there would be problems related to basic necessities, security, solvency and survival. There may be career or money worries and the subject may be temporarily unable to provide himself and his family with a secure home.

On the Apollo mount or finger a wart

might show emotional and home problems or stifled self-expression or creativity, possibly also children.

On the Mercury mount or finger there could be communication problems — the subject could be working or living alongside someone who is deliberately misunderstanding him.

On the thumb the subject would be unable to exert his will; he would be frustrated.

On any *first* phalange of the fingers there would be mental anguish; on the other phalanges, practical problems.

Warts on the hand should be read according to the line or mount. If, for example, there is a wart blocking the head line, the subject will not be thinking straight and may have difficulty with work or studies.

Warts on the back of the hand suggest problems caused by others, on the palmar side, they show that the subject himself needs to make changes in his lifestyle.

Warts that appear on children's hands are not important; they have more to do with the growing process and will go away again in time.

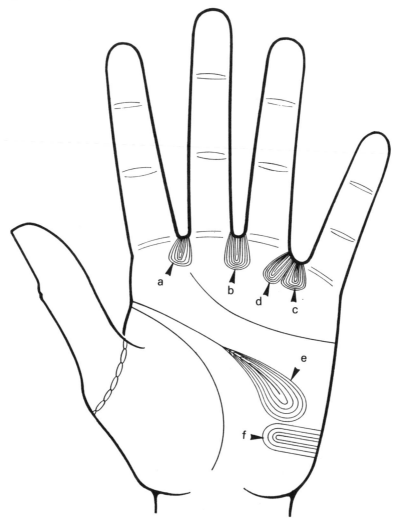

Figure 11.14 Loops

CHAPTER TWELVE

Health

WARNING: DO NOT DIAGNOSE. It is best to be a bit vague in this area of hand reading. If you really do think your subject has a problem on the way, then suggest a visit to the doctor, but make it clear that you could be completely wrong — *even if you know you are absolutely right.*

Health Checklist Guide for Hands

COLOUR
Hands should have a normal 'healthy' colour which is compatible with the race of the subject.

Pale hands	Poor circulation. If the nails stay white for a while after being pressed and the main crease lines remain pale when the hand is flexed, the subject is anaemic.
Blue/grey	Artery problems.
Yellow	Jaundice.
Red	Could be hormonal problems, glandular trouble or high blood-pressure. Red patches may indicate health problems or worries associated with the relevant area on the hand. For instance, redness around an attachment line would point to marriage problems or

something to do with children, fertility etc. Red patches may also show anger; this might be a temporary situation or the person may be habitually cross. Colds, temperatures etc. cause temporary redness.

HOT AND COLD — WET AND DRY

Hot and sweaty	This *may* point to thyroid or other glandular disorders but some people are naturally hot-handed.
Hot and dry	This *may* indicate high blood-pressure, kidney disorders, or mild fever.
Cold	This may be poor circulation, shock or,

strangely enough, the onset of a feverish ailment.

Cold and clammy   Liver sluggish.

Cold patches   Uneven circulation, possibly uneven heart action, especially if the temperature varies around each finger.

NB One can 'take' someone's blood pressure in the following way. Run your finger up and down the end of the heart line at the ulna side. If the line seems to be hard and is in a dip, the pressure is high; if the line is very soft, the pressure is low.

SOFT HANDS

It is normal to have soft hands in old age, otherwise it is an indication of poor health, lack of energy and a nervous, fearful nature. When you see hands like these, look further for specific ailments. There may be a lack of protein through bad eating-habits. The digestion system needs some kind of rhythm, so missed meals may account for this. Vegetarians usually have softer hands than meat-eaters and hands also become softer during pregnancy, so bear this in mind when looking at them.

APPEARANCE OF THE SKIN

Smooth, satiny, shiny skin points to overactivity of the thyroid gland. Ask the subject to spread the hand out and then watch to see if there is a fine trembling. Rough, coarse, dry, cold hands with brittle nails are a sign of an underactive thyroid gland.

NAILS AND HEALTH (Fig. 12.1)

LATERAL RIDGES

A shock to the system — this could be medical or emotional. A heavy indentation on all or most of the nails shows a heavy jolt to the body which may be the result of an operation or even a bereavement. Nails

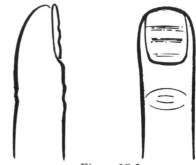

Figure 12.1

take around six to eight months to grow out depending on the state of health, therefore it is possible to date a recent incident fairly accurately. Ridges which pile up one after another like waves running onto a sea shore show repeated shocks, therefore a period of sustained trauma. Ridges on the thumb show menstrual problems in a woman's hand. On either sex, these can show prolonged anxiety and frustration.

LONGITUDINAL RIDGES (Fig. 12.2)

Figure 12.2

These show a number of complaints but the most important is some problem relating to bones and their surroundings, such as cartilage, muscles, tendons and ligaments. There may be rheumatism, slipped discs, old injuries which still leave a mark or strains and swellings of one kind or another. These are quite easy to map nail by nail. Another sign of rheumatism is a thickened third phalange on the Jupiter fingers.

Thumb	Problems with the back, also neck and head, especially if the Jupiter nail is grooved as well. The right hand shows trouble on the right side of the spine, the left shows problems on the left. Lower-back pain would affect most of the thumb nail but leave the centre section a little clearer; upper-back pain is shown by grooves and ridges which are heavier near the centre. Please bear in mind that thumbs are easily damaged, so do not confuse an accident to the nail with some awful illness!
Jupiter	Back and neck; this is usually accompanied by ridges on the thumb.
Saturn	Shoulders, rib cage, pelvis, hips.
Apollo	Arms, hands, legs, feet.
Mercury	Forearms, hands, lower legs, ankles, feet.

An isolated patch of ridging is more likely to show a break or injury. If the ridging is sharp and clear, the injury would be recent; if it is rather faded, it may be an echo from the past.

OTHER PROBLEMS ASSOCIATED WITH NAILS (Fig. 12.3)

Figure 12.3

TINY NAILS
Stomach, bladder and kidneys. If these nails seem to just sit on the finger, and the fingers are tapered or pointed, the subject is easily fatigued. He or she may have heart troubles, diabetes or may have some sort of glandular condition that leads to obesity.

'WATCHGLASS' OR 'HIPPOCRATIC' NAILS (Fig. 12.4)

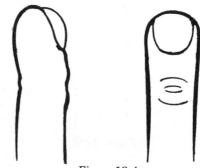

Figure 12.4

These nails bulge upwards in the middle and turn under at the end. They show a shortage of oxygen in the blood due to lung or heart damage; if the fingers are also clubbed at the end, the lungs are under severe pressure. This was traditionally a sign of tuberculosis; it may also be an indication of lung cancer or emphysema. If the lung/heart problem is temporary, the nails will grow back to normal once the trouble has gone; but if there is scarring on the lungs, the end of the Jupiter and Saturn finger will always curl round the end of the finger slightly. This curl effect is a common sight on the hands of older people who have smoked for many years. It shows that there is some damage to the periphery of the lungs.

SPOON-SHAPED NAILS (Fig. 12.5)

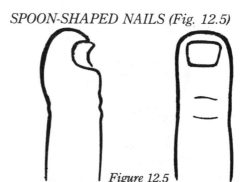

Figure 12.5

Nutritional deficiencies, underactive thyroid, also brain damage.

SLIGHTLY TURNED UNDER NAILS
(Fig. 12.6)

Figure 12.6

Emphysema, asthma, damage caused by smoking. If the subject gives up smoking, the nails eventually uncurl.

CHEWED NAILS
Nerves or a missing trace element in the diet.

WHITE SPOTS
This shows some sort of vitamin or mineral deficiency. It could be shortage of calcium or magnesium but is often a sign of lack of the vitamins associated with sunshine as these seem to show up on a great many hands in late spring. They can also be a sign of anxiety and depression.

MOONS: TOO BIG OR MISSING
Heart problems; can also show a low level of libido.

'TUNNEL NAILS' *(Fig. 12.7)*

Figure 12.7

If the end of the Mercury nail looks like this, there is spine trouble.

OVERGROWTH OF SKIN AROUND NAILS
Psoriasis.

HEALTH INDICATIONS ON THE MOUNTS

Redness on the percussion shows glandular, especially thyroid, problems and may indicate blood-pressure trouble. Redness plus fragmented lines, grilles and odd marks on Neptune shows problems with the uterus or pregnancy; on Luna and upper Mars, diabetes or possibly kidney disorders. A grille on Mercury indicates a sluggish liver. Grilles on the plain of Mars indicate liver and kidney problems.

The axial triradii (Fig. 12.9) of a healthy person is located directly above the wrist (see Fig 12.8). If it is misplaced this would be symptomatic of heart disease.

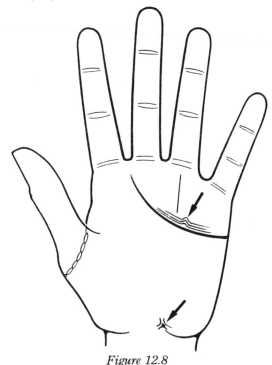

Figure 12.8

If the area around the heart line under Mercury and Apollo, where illustrated, is hard to the touch, with lines running along the heart line which are 'pushed' up by the hard lumpy area, there will be heart problems (see Fig. 12.8).

Dots, warts and even patches of eczema might point to problems in various parts of the body, otherwise the mounts do not tell us much about health.

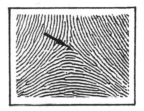

Figure 12.9

Lines and Health

The area around the attachment lines and child lines offers information related to reproduction; this is discussed in Chapter 9 and later in this chapter on page 142.

Dots and indentations on lines produce a 'whirlpool' effect sucking energies down from the lines they appear on. Bars, crosses, breaks all indicate problems, setbacks and/or health problems. Islands are often health problems but also practical and emotional difficulties — but very often these troubles are interlinked. Dots on the heart line, near the percussion, show the onset of a heart attack.

HEALTH AND THE HEART LINE
If this area is very messy, fletched and islanded, there could be a problem with the miocardium or the heart valves.

LIFE LINE
A heavily-dotted life line shows spinal disorders; one or two dots might indicate a recent operation or other shock to the system. The main purpose of marks on the life line seems to be to 'date' health problems rather than specifically identify them.

Treat the life line as a spine with the top end (near the head line) as the neck area and the bottom end as the base. Very small islands show spine damage. A large egg-shaped island near Neptune shows impending disease which may turn out to be cancer. If you think you have spotted this, please keep the information to yourself; be

wise *after* the event. It is better to be kind than to be clever in this case.

RASCETTES
These are traditionally supposed to indicate the length of life, each rascette being supposed to represent thirty years; therefore, three nice clear rascettes are said to equal ninety years of life. It is true, however, that strong rascettes *do* show generally good health but it is the topmost rascette — the one which is actually on the palm of the hand — which is the most important. If this rascette is straight and clear the health will be good; if it loops upwards into the hand there could be trouble. In a woman's hand this shows trouble with the womb. If the loop is full of strange little marks, there could be menstrual troubles or the subject may have recently had a hysterectomy. If the area is 'bitsy' and reddish, she may well be pregnant or have recently given birth!

A rascette will loop up, break and start to come to pieces if the lungs are being destroyed by cigarettes etc. If the subject gives up smoking, the line grows back. Look also for an island on the heart line (see Chapter 7).

SASHA'S COMMENT
Three years ago, my top rascettes were disintegrating, especially the one on the right hand. At that time I was smoking thirty cigarettes a day. Since giving up, the rascettes on the left hand are as good as

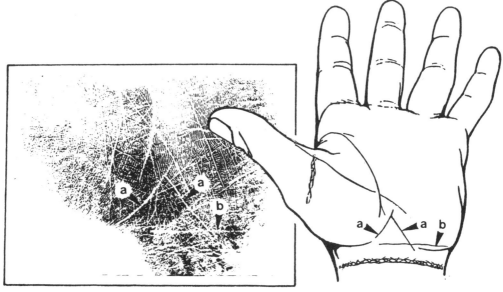

Figure 12.10

new and the right is well on the way.

UPPER RASCETTE (Fig. 12.10)

The topmost rascette (b) sometimes shows the condition of the womb. The marks come and go quite quickly as the situation changes. The characteristic tent-shaped formation shown in the print (a) means that there is, or has been some problem. In this case, the lady to whom the print belongs, has had two children by ceasarian section. This kind of formation can 'arrive' during pregnancy and gradually disappear after the womb has settled down again. If there is a triangle formation full of scattered bits of lines and the area has a reddish tinge, the subject may be in the early stages of pregnancy or possibly getting over a sterilization operation or some other womb disturbance.

HEAD LINE

BREAKS

Accidents and injuries to the head. If these are not too serious, or were averted in some way, there will be a clearly-marked square of protection around the break (see Chapter 7).

CHAINS

Under the Saturn mount, these indicate headaches and migraine. Chaining can also be caused by the 'rat in the trap' syndrome, i.e. a person whose life is frustrating and unhappy, but who has not the courage and initiative to change things for himself. Islands here relate to eyes — the subject usually wears (or needs) spectacles.

'SUGAR TONGS' ON THE PERCUSSION (Fig. 12.11)

Figure 12.11

A small formation shaped like a pair of sugar tongs which enters the hand from the percussion and 'grabs' at the end of the head line shows insomnia. Insomniacs tend to have 'full' hands (see Chapter 1).

HEART LINE
The area of the heart line which lies under the Mercury finger is almost exclusively to do with health. About the only exception to this is the fact that chaining here could point to difficult relationships in youth. In this case, there will be evidence at the start of all the other lines.

ISLANDS NEAR THE PERCUSSION
Dots indicate a pending heart attack! An island on the heart line between Mercury and Apollo shows lung trouble. Dots on either side of the island show stress on the lungs. A 'dent' in the line here indicates lung problems.

ISLANDS UNDER MERCURY
These indicate strain on the breathing, throat and bronchial tubes etc. if found near the Apollo end. A dot at either end of the island or a dark colouration is a sure indication of lung trouble. A long, rather 'lined', island here often indicates dental problems.

'FEATHERING'
If the heart line in this area shows a feathered effect, rather like the fletch end of an arrow, there will be some hardening of the arteries, possibly a tendency to develop angina.

ISLANDS UNDER SATURN
Problems with hearing.

DOTS
These show current acute problems, also inflammatory conditions. A well-marked dot on this section of the heart line shows severe strain on the heart. If the condition is cured by an operation, the dot develops a ring round it and the whole sequence gradually fades away.

Health Line (see Chapter 10)

In itself this line does not seem to have much to do with sickness, ailments etc., but it does show someone who is *interested* in health, either his own or that of others. A person who makes a point of eating the right things, takes exercise and lives a good clean life in order to maintain good health will have a health line. There *is* information to be gained about childbirth on the health line, especially down at the Luna end, but this fades some few years after the children have been born. The information would be breaks, islands or stars which show difficulty in giving birth. Clean 'sections' of line at this point show normal healthy childbirth.

People who work with the sick, look after sick relatives or go in for spiritual healing have a health line and this glows redly for about an hour after they finish their task.

TASSELLED ENDINGS ON THE LINES
On head and life lines these show illness during the later stages of life. On the head line, this may be the onset of senility (or extreme brain strain from writing palmistry books!)

FADED OR BLANK PATCHES ON THE LINES (ESPECIALLY THE LIFE LINE)
Illness or emotional shock. An old schoolfriend of Sasha's used to have a faded patch on the life line that amounted to a gap; this girl had had TB during childhood. The patch has long since mended itself and the life line is now clear. Some years ago, a young client of ours looked after her younger brother and nursed her dying mother. Towards the latter stages of

her mother's life, the grandmother came to stay and help. The grandmother was a kindly person but her ideas were totally different from those of the mother and the girl herself. The young girl developed a dramatic gap in her life line at that time, but when seen a couple of years later, the break was gone. Our friend John Lindsay commented when he heard this story that a gap in the life line does seem to show that the subject feels, at some point in their life, like a square peg in a round hole.

String of Pearls

This nasty peculiarity arises when the skin ridges become broken up and badly formed. It is due to an emotionally-based disturbance of the personality. It causes severe psychological conflict. When seen in children it is not terribly important because it is part of growing up, although it does point to emotional insecurity. In adults, it is extremely important because the subject is causing too great a strain on the body due to living off the nerves. This may be caused by pushing the body beyond limits at work, or through a drink problem.

These people need counselling but unfortunately the ridge patterns (dermatoglyphics) only really show up in hand prints or directly on the hand under a very good light. A cursory glance in ordinary light will not reveal this formation.

CASE HISTORIES

HENRY, AN ALCOHOLIC (Fig. 12.12)
Henry is now forty-nine years of age. He has been married twice, the second time at the age of thirty-five (a). He has had a history of psychological and drinking problems. The 'string of pearls' is indicative of this type of problem; i.e. acidosis due to alcohol.

His short Jupiter finger (b) shows feelings of insecurity and inferiority; the curve toward Saturn shows emotional and sexual secretiveness. He finds it difficult to unwind and to be himself. There is an exceptionally flattened arch pattern (b) on three fingers and all three have many repression ridges beneath the arches. The fingers feel extremely rigid, showing a low tolerance to stress. There is also a weak thumb.

Henry has coarse skin and soft hands which show that he is unwilling ever to listen to the advice of others and that he lacks protein. His watchglass nails show heart and lung disease plus, in this case, cirrhosis of the liver. His broken life line (c) will not be able to supply enough energy to the head line. He does not know when to stop driving himself to the limit. The fate line near the life line in this case is indicative of alcoholism and dependency on others.

A line (d) can be traced from lower Mars (childhood) cutting the fate line (lack of communication) then about to cut the Apollo line which ends in a wart (e). The wart shows us that only the subject himself has the answer to his problems.

Both the Apollo and the fate lines fade out before their route is completed on the mounts at the northern end of the hand. The broken life line shows that when he reaches fifty-two years all his energies will be very low and he will be ill; the string of pearls substantiates this. There is too much stress on the nervous system and organs of the body. The grille (f) on the ulna side by the head line shows toxic waste affecting the brain.

The man needs counselling; he is at the end of his tether; the addiction has caught up with him. His wife left him two years previously (g) and now he has been turned out of the care hostel because of his drinking.

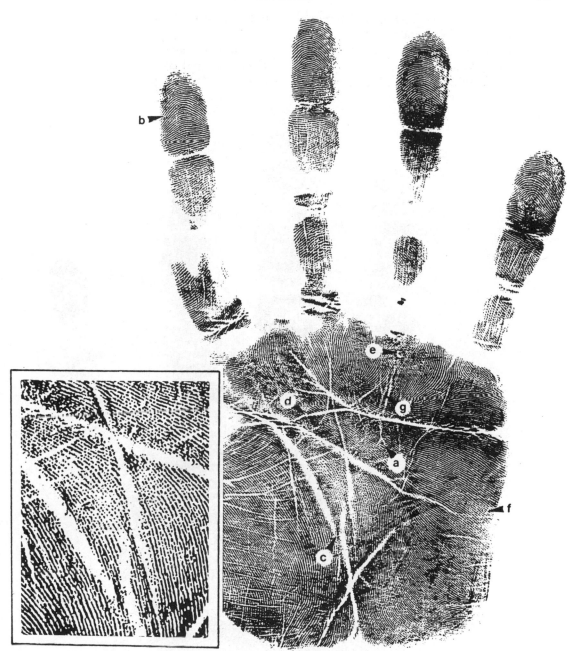

Figure 12.12 Henry

JOSIE (Fig. 12.13)

This print was taken over a rolling pin in order to get a clear centre section as the plain of Mars kept disappearing when we pressed Josie's hand directly onto the paper. We had a hilarious time taking these prints, ink and paper everywhere. In the end Josie fished out an old rolling pin that she no longer needed and we experimented with it until we perfected the technique.

After we finished printing, Josie gave me the rolling pin to keep and I have used it for awkward hands ever since. It has become a sort of lucky charm!

Josie is forty-two years of age and has had two heart attacks. All the major lines on Josie's hand, especially the life line (a), become tasselled and weak at the ends signifying a kind of 'giving up' on life. The heart line under Mercury (b) is far too

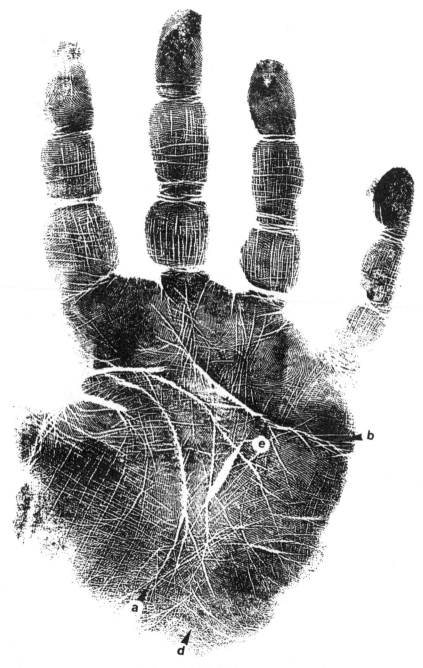

Figure 12.13 Josie

feathered for a woman of her age and the rascettes are breaking up (d). However the fate and Apollo lines reach the top of the palm which indicates a normal life span. The presence of the health line and healing striata show that she can recover well, even from severe illness.

There is a small sharply-shaped island (e) on the heart line under the Mercury/Apollo junction (which the print does not show clearly); its presence shows that there has been a severe emotional shock some time in the past. This occurred a few years ago when her husband suddenly announced that he was leaving her for another woman. Josie had had a bad time giving birth to her only child, Rachael, which probably weakened her constitution. I vaguely remember something about rheumatic fever in her childhood. If that is the case, the myocardium (the skin around the heart, enclosing the coronary arteries) would have been damaged. The trauma caused by her husband's behaviour brought on the beginnings of the angina.

It is interesting to note that there are an excessive number of lines showing up around the heart line in the area which indicates Josie's late thirties. This is typical evidence of an energy rhythm (see Chapter 6). There was more nervous energy stored up in her body than she could cope with at that time. This build-up of emotional and physical energy could have been released through work or exercise but Josie's rheumatism prevented her from exercising and she gave up work at that time due to 'nerves'.

Josie is now forty-two years old and would be the first to agree that she is very overweight. Her face is pretty and her nature is lovely but she is too fat for her health.

Josie now leads a very quiet life with her sixteen year old daughter. They are surrounded by good friends and relatives, plus visitors from London bearing printing ink and so forth. Josie knows that Rachael will inevitably grow up and leave her but my guess is that they will always remain close. If Josie continues to live quietly, enjoying her hobbies of sewing and craft-work, she should have a long — if not very exciting — life.

DIABETES AND EARLY DEATH (Fig. 12.14)

Figure 12.14

The clue to diabetes is a pattern of fine lines coming away at an angle from the fate line and re-appearing on Pluto. These fine lines are sometimes called a grille and may form a cross somewhere in that area. The print shown in Fig. 12.14 is that of a woman with a short life line. This woman died in her late fifties at the age where the life line terminates; if she had lived past that point, the life line would move over to touch the fate line and, in this case because the fate line is very fretted here, she would have been incapacitated. As it was, she was able to tend to the needs of her family until the very last.

AN INDICATION OF CANCER (Fig. 12.15)

If there is a cluster of small globules with a transparent sheen, either yellow or flesh coloured, on the edge of the hand — the radial side of the mount of Venus — this can be a sign of cancer; but one must look for other signs, such as blue islands on the heart line etc., to substantiate this claim.

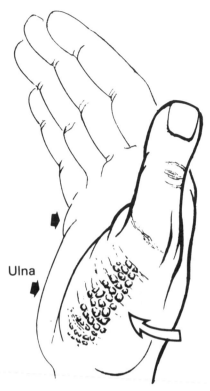

Ulna

Figure 12.15

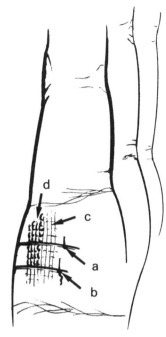

Figure 12.16

REPRODUCTION AND HEALTH ON THE CHILD LINES

MISCARRIAGE (Fig. 12.16a)

This is shown by a red dot or a pinprick hole on the attachment line below the child line. A short stunted child line will sometimes show miscarriage or a stillborn child.

ABORTION (Fig. 12.16b)

This is similar to miscarriage. There will be a small crater on the attachment line beneath the child line with a small blue vein line coming from it.

HYSTERECTOMY (Fig. 12.16c): SMEAR TEST (Fig. 12.16d)

This is shown by a lot of fine vertical lines covering the area of the attachment lines; these also point to health in the reproduction area. If the skin between the lines appears to glisten or take on a transparent sheen then the subject should be advised to take a smear test. NB Be careful! Do not frighten your subject. Admit that you are most likely to be mistaken, but suggest a visit to the doctor anyway, just to eliminate any possible health doubts.

MORE INFORMATION ON REPRODUCTION AND HEALTH (Fig. 12.10)

If the subject is particularly interested in matters relating to health and reproduction, the palmist must also look at the part of the hand at the bottom of the palm, immediately above the rascettes on the mount of Neptune. This gives some more information about pregnancy and the state of a woman's womb at the time of the reading.

CHAPTER THIRTEEN

Case Histories

How to Approach a Reading (Case History)

'Marie' — an actress (Fig. 13.1)

Marie has appeared on the stage and in television in many different roles. At the age of twenty-one she had pneumonia very badly and nearly died.

(a) Island on the heart line (lung trouble).
(b) Illness island.
(c) Life line almost parted.

Due to her own great efforts she recovered, although the lungs took a long time to restore themselves to normal health.

(d) Double life line.
(e) Island with effort line.

At the age of twenty-nine she married.

(f) Strong new Apollo line going to the fate line.

Her acting career prospered and her marriage faltered.
By the age of thirty-eight she was divorced.

(g) Fate line moves to radial side.

(i) Split in fate line with an influence line which can be traced from the family line to the attachment lines.

She then married a man in the same profession as herself.

(h) Coming together.

(j) Common interests.

This marriage too ran into difficulties, also her career took a dive.

(k) Parallel line with a split (age fifty-three).

She spent a good deal of time waiting at home for the telephone to ring with offers of work. Meanwhile she took an open university course.

(f) Apollo line showing a return to home life.

(m) Hobbies and interests.

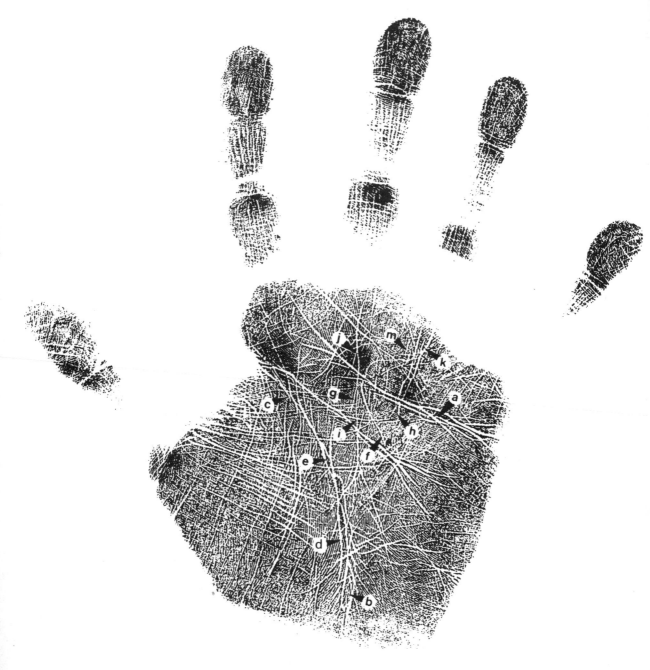

Figure 13.1 Marie

An Ordinary Woman: Chris, character reading with some events (Fig. 13.2)

The tracery of fine lines on Chris's hand shows that she is sensitive by nature and was feeling a touch nervous at the time that the print was taken. Her long straight Jupiter finger which pulls away slightly from Saturn shows that she likes to think things out for herself. The head line which is lightly tied to the life line with a cat's cradle effect (a), plus the effort lines rising almost from the start of her life, tell us that she was not too happy as a child and found it hard to concentrate while at school. Those early effort lines suggest idealism. The gap between the Saturn and Apollo fingers shows some inner rebelliousness. This kind of person always has difficulty during childhood because they do not conform and childhood is all about behaving and conforming.

In the lower zone of the hand, the life and fate lines are separate but there is a heavy bar artificially tying them together (b). This bar seems to be imposed upon the other lines. This shows some confusion brought about by Chris's early need for freedom as against the actual restrictiveness of her upbringing. I would guess that there was a heavy religious influence in the parental home. This restrictiveness and 'correct-ness' of behaviour being imposed is reinforced by the line which trails down from the head line (c) showing that she married someone who was considered 'suitable' by her family and the society in which she lived, rather than choosing someone for mental and physical attraction.

The clearly-marked Apollo line which has its source at the life line (d) shows the desire for a stable and comfortable home; the peacock's eye on the Apollo finger gives taste and refinement, possibly artistic and musical appreciation as well. Her home must be an attractive place. The marks inside the Apollo finger (e) and the

'shadow' lines which accompany the life line (f) tell us that Chris may be slightly mystical, even psychic. The loop of imagin-ation and memory (g) on the Mars/Luna mount and the fairly full mount of Neptune give sensitivity and some understanding of people's unconscious motives; this is heightened by the fragmented girdle of Venus. This sensitivity and imaginativeness make her kindly and understanding.

The head line bounces just on top of the large loop (g) giving her a good memory. She seems to be imaginative in her thinking rather than logical due to the northerly placement of the memory/imagination loop. The 'waisted' second phalange of the thumb causes her to question things in order to find a logical explanation for the things that she can 'feel'. The turned up end of the head line gives business ability; the full mount of Mercury and slightly inward-turning Mercury finger give shrewdness and acumen. Chris has no loop of serious intent (h), therefore she would find it hard to discipline her thoughts unless there was practical reason for doing so (hence the slim second phalange of the thumb).

The lines which enter the fate line at the age of twenty-two (i) show marriage after a long serious relationship. The long line entering the fate line and travelling to the life line shows that she could live close to her parents. The flick away from the fate line (j) a year or two later shows an ending and a decision. This decision to end some-thing related to an affair which she had during the second year of marriage! At this point Chris 'grew up', gave up work and started a family. The doubling of the head and heart lines and life line from the age of around twenty-five to her late thirties shows confusion and split-mindedness

Figure 13.2

about her duties toward her family. The line which travels toward and becomes parallel to the fate line (k) at about the age of thirty shows her going back to work again and splitting her energies between the family and her job. Note the presence of secretiveness marks on lower Mars and northern Venus (l). The long attachment line with the slight companion lines above and below (m) show that she solved the problems of being married to someone not entirely to her taste by having other interests; these interests may have included other liaisons. There is also a hint that she has been 'widowed' in the past! This is shown by the bubble of shock (n) on the heart line and the influence line just where the heart line begins to split and bend (o). Chris's forked head line shows that she can be different people in different places, i.e. dedicated housewife, mother, business woman, worker, artist and entertainer (long Apollo finger with peacock-shaped whorl).

The segment of the girdle of Venus under the Apollo finger (p) plus the long head line and long first phalanges tell us that Chris is intelligent and likes to learn. She cultivates the company of those whom she considers to be older and wiser. Her loop of humour (q) shows her to be an attractive and spontaneous personality. The forked heart line shows that Chris wants to relate (r) to men but at the same time remain detached. She chooses her men for qualities which she finds socially rather than sexually attractive; she must be able to feel proud of them, because such a strong part of the heart line goes straight out to the lower part of the mount of Jupiter (s).

FIG. 13.3

Although personally independent, she is both genuinely caring and also has a peculiar desire to control others by giving. This is shown by the flaky health line (a) which partly joins the attachment line. The flakes which run down from the heart line

to the head line show some measure of uncertainty about her sexual nature. She seems to be 'normal' (i.e. heterosexual) but could have some difficulty in relating to or trusting men. The upper part of the heart line (b) reaches into the ring of Solomon; this shows that Chris identifies herself as being a lovable person by helping, obliging and caring — possibly in a slightly maternal way. She would probably prefer to make sure her man was well fed than well bedded. Her caring identity is so strong that she probably does a lot for the young, old, sick or for animals. She needs a creative job with a caring outlet.

Chris's mind is restless and ambitious — this is shown by the slightly islanded, forked and flaky head line plus her ambitiously high mount of Jupiter with its triradius and the whorls on her finger tips. This battles slightly with her need for domestic harmony as shown by the life line which curves round Venus. Chris seems to have little desire to travel as the life line stays close to home, there are few travel lines and she has an inwards dent on the lower precussion at Pluto (c). The small sharply-rising line on the edge of Jupiter (d) shows that she can make money for herself at a pinch.

There is an influence line crossing the fate line (e) at the age of forty-five and a bend in one of the Apollo line flakes which seems to show a new job very near the home. There is also a redefinition of relationships at this point shown by the breaks in the Apollo and fate lines (f). Chris seems to have come into money in her early fifties. This may have been as a result of a legacy which is shown by the new addition to the fate line (g) which begins to travel to Apollo, plus the fact that the Apollo lines seems to start on or inside the life line. This shows an increasing ability to obtain self-expression from life rather than just to live and earn money in order to put the family's food on the table. The upward flick at the end of the head line (h) shows her developing interest in business. There is some evidence of a death; this is shown by the shock island (i) on the heart line and the slight 'snapping' of the heart (j) with an influence line just at that point. The evidence is corroborated by the position of the influence line (k) indicating the death of a relative or close friend. This could be how she has gained her freedom and found the money for a new start!

Chris's attitude is becoming gradually more adventurous now as shown by the outward flick at the bottom of the life line plus the rising optimism of the head and heart lines.

She certainly has had some sexual problems to sort out. This is partly because of her 'caring' attitude to love and also her preference for friendship rather than close sexual relationships. The majority of the heart line travels straight across to Jupiter with slight downward flicks (l). The long drooping attachment line shows a long-standing attachment to one man (m). This could be a boyfriend, but is just as likely to be the friendly suitable husband who stays nicely in the background while she explores her deeper feelings elsewhere! The drooping lines which fall from this attachment line (m) show that he frustrates her and leans upon her in some way, but her caring nature can cope with this.

One of these long drooping attachment lines shows that in her fifties she will have to look after elderly or sick relatives in or near the home. There are two branch lines going toward the home area (n) at the beginning of two vertical lines which suddenly end, thus showing the death of the elderly person.

There seem to have been business partnerships in the past as shown by the line entering the heart line (o). There will be others in the future as shown by the influence line entering and then crossing

the head line (p). Chris's health is basically good although her lungs may be a little weak (q), therefore she should have plenty of life ahead of her to live and enjoy.

Just one final point — I am sure she likes dancing. Now is this coming to me clairvoyantly or can I see it on the hand? Let us think for a moment. The long Apollo finger and Apollo line show artistry, the width across the Luna/Venus area shows an active person, the upward curve of the heart line shows sensuality (although in this case not sexuality), the angle of rhythm (r) is strongly marked and the thumb is spokeshaved which implies some desire to be popular. The restriction lines show that too much responsibility bores her and she needs to get away and have some fun on occasion. Active fun with her own sex, movement, music and a love of life seems to me to make her into a sportswoman or a good amateur dancer.

NOTE SASHA'S TALE
After writing most of this piece, I was put in touch with Chris who wrote and confirmed my findings. There were a couple of minor adjustments to be made and some information to be added. Chris said in her letter that the most important factor in her life has been the restriction placed upon her by her demanding mother who has lived with Chris on and off all her life. Mother is still alive now at the age of ninety-two, still in good fettle and still getting her own way!

I was confused by the death and the legacy but Chris explained that a close friend had died and left her some money which she has indeed used in order to start a new and enjoyable business partnership. Chris also confirmed that she still *likes* her husband, she always did. She worries about him and wants him to be happy, but they no longer live together.

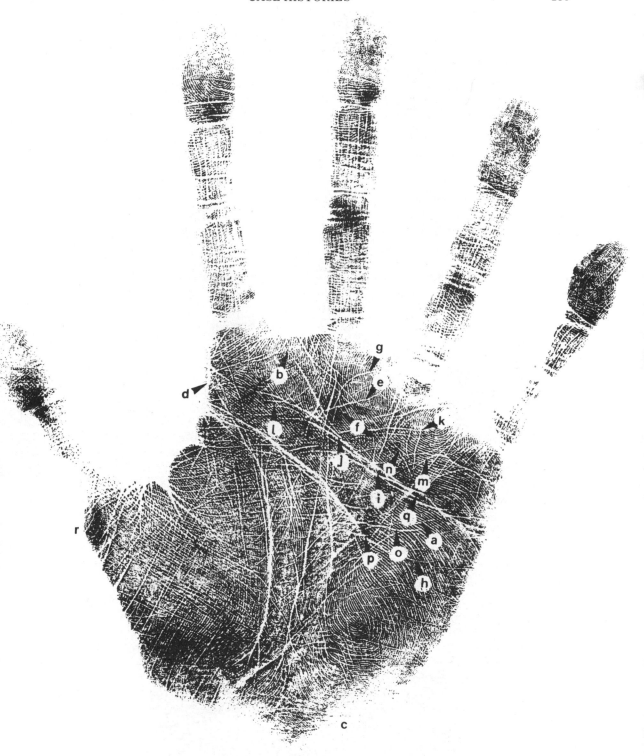

Figure 13.3

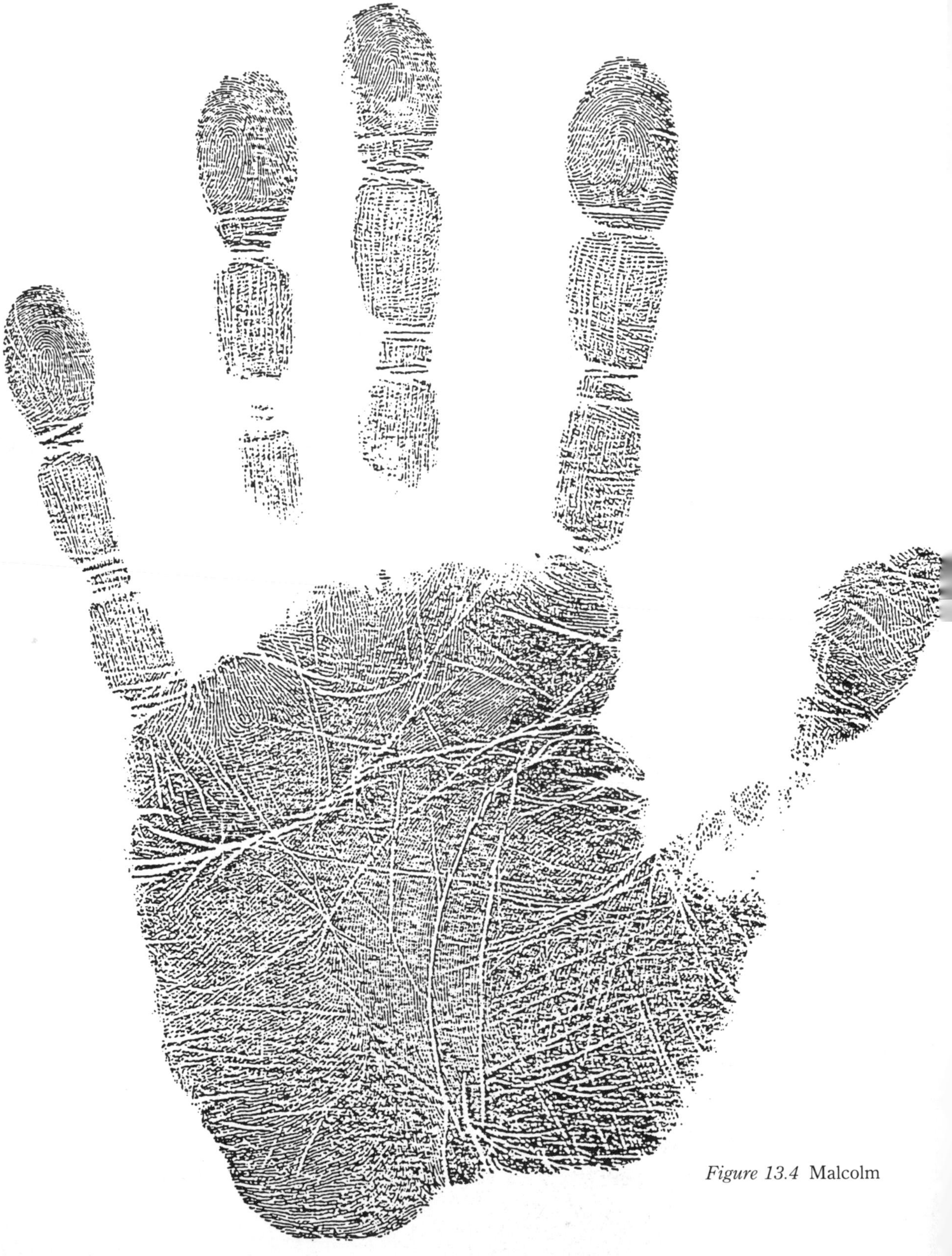

Figure 13.4 Malcolm

The Anatomy of a Partnership

MALCOLM (Fig. 13.4)
and SASHA (Fig. 13.5)

Many people form partnerships for one purpose or another and often, especially in the world of creative achievement, nothing much comes of them. Why therefore did this one work? What fate chose to bring us together and what special alchemy made the whole thing function so well?

We have supplied our own prints at this point as a kind of epilogue to the book so that you, the reader, can work out for yourself why we both choose to make our living by working as self-employed hand readers and why we found it so easy to collaborate on this project when, heaven knows, neither of us is easy going. We have not given you any clues with this reading, no carefully-placed letters to follow. We are leaving it to you to make your own assessments and to test your own hand-reading abilities.

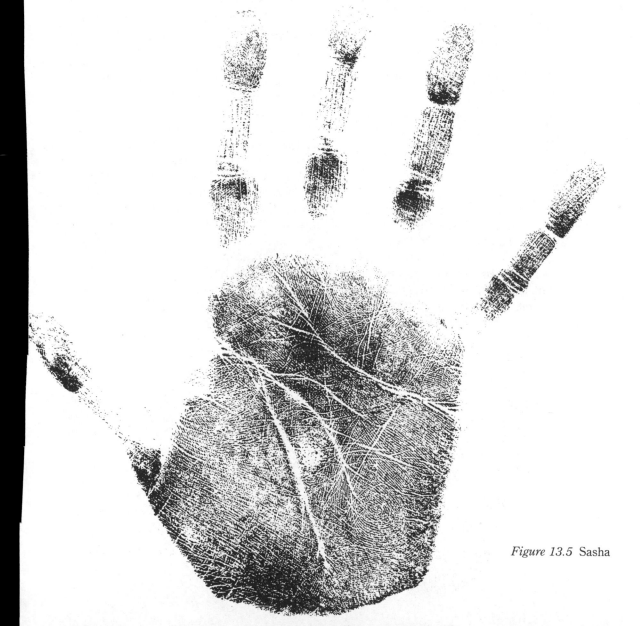

Figure 13.5 Sasha

Malcolm and I met in 1984 at the Festival of Mind, Body and Spirit at Olympia in London. We started chatting to each other about palmistry and found that we shared similar views. We both said how much we would like to write a book which swept away the ancient cobwebs and gave hand readers an original view.

I knew that I could write but I had no idea that Malcolm could illustrate; Malcolm did not know about word processing or realize that I had my own machine. It was only when we began serious discussions that it became clear that between us we had all the skills necessary for the job.

As we got to know one another, we discovered that we have similar tastes and a firm friendship as well as a working partnership began to evolve.

A PALMIST'S VIEW OF SASHA AND MALCOLM

'Let not thy left hand know what thy right hand doeth.'

THE SIMILARITIES

Both hands are fairly long. Men's hands usually have fewer fine lines than women's but Malcolm's hands are quite 'full' for a man's while Sasha's are also pretty 'full'. This shows us to be sensitive to hurt and able to link in with and understand the hurts of others. Neither hands have clear-cut main lines, all the lines are heavily branched, except for Sasha's heart line which is reasonably clear. This shows that we are both swept up by changing circumstances from time to time and both have many-faceted personalities. Both hands are long and square with a long palm. The mounts are rather flat. They both have life lines which reach outwards; curved, sloping head lines with branches; curved heart lines with girdles of Venus. Both show confusion at the start of the head and life lines. This shows that our early lives showed difficulties. We share the same features of long strong thumbs, restriction and responsibility lines on the fingers and thumbs, family interference lines and only one strong attachment line. The need to please and to help other people is shown by loops of humour, rings of Solomon, health lines and healing striata.

THE DIFFERENCES

Malcolm is left-handed. Malcolm's hands are large with long fingers showing a love of detail and the long third phalanges show that detailed work comes easily to him. Sasha's hand is relatively small with a long palm and fairly short fingers, the longest phalange being the first. This shows her speedy grasp of an overall situation, ability to plan and organize. Malcolm's life line follows fairly well around Venus although there is a more adventurous outward movement in its latter stages, plus a new home situation to come. Sasha's leaves Venus for pastures new at about the age of forty-two. Sasha's head line is more deeply marked and has a branch below plus an extra head line above. Malcolm's is finer but *is almost exactly the same shape including the branch* but does not have the extra upper head line. Malcolm's heart line shows a strong line of noncommunication and a heavy girdle of Venus above. Sasha's heart line is fairly clear but ends almost at the top of the hand on Jupiter. They both have the C section of the girdle showing the need to communicate with like-minded people; they both can become intellectually immersed in what they are doing.

NB The astrologers among you might like to note that Malcolm has the Sun and Moon in Pisces with Leo rising. Sasha has the Sun in Leo, the Moon in Pisces and Gemini rising. Both of us are therefore creative, proud of our achievements, humorous and communicative; as well as being moody, sarcastic and critical of both ourselves and others.

Index